Sewing Big

Sewing Big

Fashion Advice and Sewing Tips for Larger Sizes

Elizabeth J. Musheno

VNR VAN NOSTRAND REINHOLD COMPANY

NEW YORK   CINCINNATI   TORONTO   LONDON   MELBOURNE

Printed in the United States of America
Designed by Rose Delia Vasquez

Published by Van Nostrand Reinhold Company Inc.
135 West 50th Street
New York, NY 10020

Van Nostrand Reinhold Publishing
1410 Birchmount Road
Scarborough, Ontario M1P 2E7, Canada

Van Nostrand Reinhold Australia Pty. Ltd.
17 Queen Street
Mitcham, Victoria 3132, Australia

Van Nostrand Reinhold Company Limited
Molly Millars Lane
Wokingham, Berkshire, England

16   15   14   13   12   11   10   9   8   7   6   5   4   3   2   1

Library of Congress Cataloging in Publication Data
Musheno, Elizabeth J.
  Sewing big.

  Includes index.
  1. Dressmaking.   2. Sewing.   3. Clothing and dress.   I. Title.
TT560.M8   646.4'304   81-23097
ISBN 0-442-21907-5   AACR2

Acknowledgments

In putting together a book about fashion selection and sewing for the large woman, the logical approach is to seek the assistance of people who are dedicated to helping her look good and lending moral support. These people gave freely of their time and talents:

Philip Verderosa, quality control manager, and Richard Gilbert, advertising director, of Roaman's, specialists in large and half-size retail and mail order ready-to-wear fashions.

Pat Swift of Plus Woman, a New York model agency.

Lisbeth Fisher, executive secretary of the National Association to Aid Fat Americans, which has many local chapters across America.

Contents

Getting started. Determining your height category. Determining your figure type. A six-step figure analysis: Rectangular, Full, Round hip, Large bust, Square, or Round figure.

Design lines. Garment balance and proportion. Basic dress styles. Necklines. Tops, overblouses, and jackets. Skirts. Pants. Fashion lines by figure type (chart).

Understanding the pattern. Wearing ease. Style ease. Fitted garments, Semifitted, Slightly-fitted, Loosely-fitted. And now it is you! Measuring for undergarments. Measuring for your pattern size. How to determine your pattern size. Pattern styles for special sizes: Dresses, Pants, Skirts, Tops and overblouses, Jackets, Coats. Fashionable styles for you: Rectangular figure, Full, round hip, Large bust, Square, and Round.

Understanding Color. Evaluating Color. How to find your best color. Putting colors together. Using color as an accent. Color for an optical illusion. Hair color and style. Cosmetics.

Preface

If you are the kind of large and lovely woman who wants to look and feel good in today's fashions, and you enjoy sewing, this book has been written especially for you. It was inspired by my second daughter, Adelade, who asked me to write this one for her. As a young wife and mother, with a young, executive husband, she wants to be stylishly dressed, even though her figure is ample. Adelade knows how to sew but does not have a good working knowledge of the basics needed to select patterns with becoming lines; fabric in complementary colors, and color combinations, or surface and texture treatments; and she was not sure about accessorizing her newly sewn fashions. I am sure there are many women like my daughter—wholesome, attractive, clever, and capable—who want to be the best dressed large-sized woman for every activity in their busy lives. I want every big woman to be able to wear

carefully selected and sewn outfits appropriate to her height and figure and to develop a fashion image that is an expression of her personality. Clothing has always been a problem for large women, and I hope you will find the solutions to your special problems with the aid of this book.

Dedicated to all the big and beautiful women I have known, beginning with my mother. This book is for all women—young and chunky, middle-aged and plump, older and stout, who wear half-sizes 14½ to 24½ or women's sizes 38 to 60—who want to be smartly dressed and find sewing an outlet for their creativity and want to develop the skills and aesthetic sensitivity required to make up a total fashion look. The large women of today no longer accept dowdy or matronly looking clothing. Instead, they are asking for and getting attractive up-to-date fashions. Now, I would like to help them tie it all together in a pleasing manner. The happiness experienced by women who sew well-made garments, often receiving unsolicited compliments, more than makes up for the time-consuming aspects of the craft. They have expressed their feelings and ideas in the same way an artist does when he or she chooses colors, textures, and forms to create a work of art.

The object of this book is to give enough information on figure types, design lines, pattern selection, color, fabric, sewing tips, accessories, and alterations so that the big woman, regardless of age, can intelligently select and sew appropriate fashions for her figure. I hope that every reader will gain a comprehensive understanding of her figure so that she can make proper use of design lines and controlled balance and proportion for each garment sewn. Basic design silhouettes, such as skimmer, empire, or sheath and fashion details, such as necklines and sleeves, as well as many other familiar clothing types, are explained. The overview of patterns should aid you in the selection of the ones most appropriate for specific occasions. Studying the color guide will lead to exploration

of colorful fabrics for each season's wardrobe with a new comprehension of the broad range of possibilities suitable for each figure type.

Sewing these personally selected fashions is a breeze, with the many adaptations shown for your favorite silhouettes. Clothing is not all there is to fashion; so you will learn how to use accessories to balance a costume and keep proportions scaled to your figure. When you find the need to purchase ready-made garments, you will be able to select the most flattering item, using the information assembled in this book. Basic alteration methods that the larger figure may require are given so you will always be well-groomed, whether you sew or purchase a garment.

Before you buy another fashion item, whether it is a pattern or a pair of shoes, I hope you will read chapters 1 through 5 and chapter 8. These chapters will acquaint you with what is needed for experimentation and will aid you in evaluating each aspect of fashion and sewing as it relates to your figure. Chapter 1 should help you make an honest evaluation of your figure. Chapters 2 and 3 put fashion design lines into their proper perspective. You will

learn how seams, hems, necklines, and closures are used by designers to maintain balance and proportion. These fundamentals are reflected in the patterns available for the ample figure, along with a thorough explanation of fit as it pertains to various silhouettes. Chapters 4 and 5 will help you make fashion-wise decisions for becoming colors and fabrics that will work for your figure. In chapter 8 you will learn how to use accessories to help preserve the balance and proportion of each ensemble. The remaining chapters will be most helpful when you want to sew variations into your favorite patterns or when you require alterations on ready-to-wear garments.

I am extremely grateful for the fashion and technical sketches drawn by my tall, slim, and beautiful illustrator, Marie Martin Withers. A positive attitude is the prevailing theme presented in this book. Using your imagination, and *Sewing Big*, you can make a unique contemporary fashion statement that features distinctive apparel, personally created by you for every occasion.

Introduction

The large-sized woman, who wants to sew fashionable clothes and learn how to dress with style, must first set things right in her own mind. She must accept her size, make a commitment to be the most attractively dressed woman possible, and then change her attitude about herself. *Sewing Big* will tell you what help is available, how to take inventory of what you own and what you know, and then launch you on an exciting fashion and sewing adventure.

First, accept yourself—a healthy, intelligent, vivacious woman who is no longer hung up on the allure of a skinny body. You have tried every diet and the results were always the same: the weight was soon gained back, starting you off on another guilt trip. Decide that you are no longer going to hide inside dowdy, badly fitting clothes. Instead, you will call on your inner resources to spur you to action as you investi-

gate the world of fashion sewing.

You do not need a perfect figure or have to be a small size to look sensational. There are sewing and fashion tricks that will help you look chic regardless of your size. Few women are happy with their figure! Many women who wear size 10 or smaller have problems of proportion, such as a large bust or big hips. Figure problems have plagued fashion-conscious women for years, and they require special consideration each time a new garment is purchased or sewn. I do not agree with the theory that since you are of larger than average size, you should wear anything you like, even when you know you do not look your best. I realize that if you weigh 250 pounds, you cannot expect to look much smaller with special style features or colors, but these fashion effects may be used to help you be a well-dressed big woman. This book will be a valuable tool for *every woman* who wants to dress to camouflage a figure flaw and be smartly attired in an outfit that looks balanced and in proportion with her figure. No more giving way to despair and discouragement. Accept your size and make the most of it by learning how to be a person of style.

Second, make a commitment to wear becoming clothes. The way you dress can deeply affect your well-being, instill confidence, and contribute to your achievements. You can be both big and beautiful if you are willing to spend the time and have the patience to attain the goal of every woman—to be a success under any circumstance, whether she is a student, lover, wife, mother, working woman, or all five. So much depends on the assurance that you look your best. Good grooming and attractive clothing will help you become a more poised, self-confident woman in your home, social, or business life.

Gone is the era of the hourglass figure when waist-cinching corsets were worn by every fashionable woman to create a seemingly small waist. Large-busted women no longer bind their breasts to emulate the flat-chested flapper of the Roaring Twenties. Today's woman wants comfortable, flexible clothes that allow her freedom of movement. Knowing how to interpret the shape of the figure is the foundation of all fashions for casual wear, work, and dress-up.

Third, examine your attitude about yourself. Attitude is most important when you start thinking about how to dress with distinction. When people meet you while shopping or pass you on the street (figure I–1), do they see a large, attractive, well-groomed woman wearing appropriately fashionable clothes and accessories? Or, do they see an untidy woman with unkempt hair, wearing wrinkled, baggy, and poorly fitting clothes and worn shoes?

When dressed for a special event (figure I–2), do you walk tall with self-assurance, having selected an elegant outfit and hairstyle that looks balanced and in proportion to your ample figure? Or, do you dress in a badly fitting and proportioned frock and tacky shoes, with unflattering hair, as you shuffle or waddle

Figure I–1: Appearance is important. The way you dress discloses how you feel about yourself. Learn how to dress smartly for every activity in your life.

along with your head down, hoping no one will notice you?

How do you look to others at a public gathering or a private party? Do you sit gracefully with legs crossed at the ankles or closely aligned, or do you slouch with your legs spread? A fully-formed, big woman who is willing to spend some time learning to be fashionably dressed should be cognizant of how she appears to other people, whether at home, at work, or in public. Think honestly about the fashion image you project. Every large-proportioned person should acquire an attitude of poise and a proud carriage.

Where to Find Help

It can be fun to learn ways to show off your new craft—dressing and sewing for big, beautiful you! And there are many groups ready and willing to help the nearly twenty-five million American women who wear size sixteen or larger (according to the United States Bureau of Standards) to be better dressed. At this time, you will find more help than ever when looking for something new and sensational to wear. Nonprofit self-help groups, magazines, mail-order and retail businesses, pattern companies, and fashion-model agencies are stressing the intelligence and

beauty of the ample-sized, well-groomed woman.

The National Association to Aid Fat Americans (NAAFA, P.O. Box 745, Westbury, N.Y. 11590) is a nonprofit group that seeks to increase the happiness and well-being of fat people of all ages, both men and women. The main problems of all fat people are poor self-image; the difficulty of acquiring stylish, well-fitting clothing; job and social discrimination; guilt feelings; exploitation by commercial interests; inability to buy most health and life insurance; unsympathetic treatment by many doctors; being the butt of countless jokes; and often, lack of understanding by their immediate family. In fact, fat people sometimes have trouble merely being treated like human beings who have the same needs and rights as everyone else.

NAAFA points out that there is considerable evidence that *ideal*

Figure I-2: Walk tall. Enhance a beautiful costume and hairstyle with good posture, walking gracefully. Do not slump or shuffle along in an unattractive manner. Stand tall and glide as you walk. Every large and lovely woman can acquire a regal attitude.

weight has been poorly and rigidly defined in height/weight tables, and what is fat for one person may be normal for another. They stress that a fat individual is not necessarily unhealthy; it depends on the degree of fatness and the physical characteristics of the person in question.

Even in cases where an individual would be better off weighing less, the alternative for many people is a long series of weight gains and losses—called the yo-yo syndrome—which can ruin health faster than remaining fat. Many scientists specializing in the study of weight control have made this point repeatedly.

Lisbeth Fisher, executive secretary of NAAFA says, ''Fat is an adjective, just as short, tall, thin, blonde-haired, or blue-eyed; yet society has turned it into a derogatory word. It is time for it to be put into its proper perspective.'' She went through the yo-yo syndrome for nearly eight years and then decided she would accept herself—just as she is. No more diets, no more self-incrimination. She was going to be the best looking fat woman she could be—and this should be your attitude, too. As an intelligent, sensitive woman you should be ready to make your debut as a large, attractive person.

From time to time, some of the established fashion magazines will feature a few styles for the large woman, but their concept of large is usually a size 14. Do not despair. Now the large woman has her own fashion magazine: *BBW* for big, beautiful women. Published in Los Angeles six times a year, its editor-in-chief, Carole Shaw, is a big, beautiful, and perceptive woman who knows the problems that confront the ample person. *BBW* presents fashions, along with the names of stores where they are available, and various articles designed to aid, advise, and assist its readers.

Retail stores and mail-order catalogs like Roaman's have always carried half-sizes 14½ to 24½ and women's sizes 38 to 60. These stores carry everything a large woman needs from shoes and underthings, to youthful, up-to-date clothes—including designer sportswear, daytime, and dress-up garments scaled to fit the ample figure. More recently, large department stores like Saks Fifth Avenue, Bloomingdale's, Macy's, and Gimbel's are carrying a selection of designer fashions in large sizes, along with the other standard merchandise required in these sizes. The establishments that have specialized in large sizes for years continue to cater to large and tall women exclusively, giving full attention to their every need, not just partial service.

Philip Verderosa, quality control manager of Roaman's Mail Order, Inc. says, ''Large women need all the help they can get when it comes to planning a complementary wardrobe. For so long, mail-order catalogs were the only resource for some women who wished to purchase large-sized clothing, undergarments, hosiery, and shoes, and many still use this method. We recently conducted a survey that indicated our customers want fashionable clothes in their size for every aspect of their life. Roaman's is now fitting the large woman's taste as well as her size with a young, fashionable look.''

The pattern companies have always carried some half and women's sizes, but they do not offer the wide selection available in misses' sizes. They are beginning to show more stylish and youthful garments in these sizes on larger models, but they do not always match the designs to the model's figure as well as they do for the slender models. Dressing the large woman is still in a formative stage. During the years I worked for pattern companies, some designers felt that if a woman had a thirty-inch waist she should not wear pants. Now Gloria Vanderbilt and Murjani are proving that big women can look great in jeans when everything the woman wears is in scale.

The realization that big and beautiful is a lucrative and receptive market is encouraging the production of more and better wearing apparel and accessories for every activity. It is up to you to take advantage of every type of help available and to speak up when you are not happy with the merchandise you find. Large women cannot wear clothes designed for pencil-thin models that have merely been enlarged. When a manufacturer does this, the scale of the design is all wrong. The plump body needs darts, ease, and tucks that will allow the fabric to skim over the contours, without emphasizing them, and drape gracefully.

Pat Swift of Plus Models, a model agency in New York City, conducts fashion shows across America. She says, ''More important than fashion is properly fitting clothes. Eighty percent of the women I see as prospective models or at fashion shows wear their clothes too tight. Large women are so hung up on size that they force themselves into a size they think they should wear and consequently wear clothes that are unflattering. The true thing that makes women look better is good fit. If they were given the know-how to fit and alter their clothes it would be a great saving.''

A tall, vivacious, well-proportioned woman with a rectangular figure, Pat recently modeled an elegant nightgown and peignoir and other outfits on TV's ''Real People,'' seen across America.

Pat Swift is one of the new generation of large women who refuses to be treated differently than a woman who wears a size 8. While traveling, on behalf of her business, she may challenge a manufacturer to make a jogging suit, sexy lingerie, or other timely garments for the many Plus-size women she sees each day. Or she may be heard on TV or radio talk shows expressing her annoyance with the discrimination and injustices large women face daily.

Sewing Big is meant to be a guide to fashion and sewing for large and lovely ladies, regardless of age, who are tired of wearing inappropriate clothes and like to sew. When well-dressed, a woman feels beautiful and special, and big women should acquire the fashion sense that will enable them to sew a figure-flattering wardrobe.

Take Inventory

Now is the time to take inventory of what you own and what you know. You will want to find out why you look and feel good in some garments, while others fail to make a good fashion statement. By carefully examining the style lines and design features of your most becoming outfits, you will recognize these same silhouettes as you read this book. You will also learn what was wrong with the ones that lacked distinction.

Why not be your own fashion coordinator? Keep a file or a notebook where you can record data pertinent to your hair, face, and figure. Make it your cookbook of fashion and collect recipes for stylish and flattering fashions that are appropriate to your life-style and you. Start collecting examples of garments you think are attractive from newspapers and magazines. Get to know your style preferences. The total garment may not appeal to you, but you may like the neck treatment, or the center-front interest on a skirt style may be a variation of your favorite silhouette. Or perhaps it is a hairstyle, hat, jewelry, or other accessories that will add special interest to an outfit in your present wardrobe. With the help of this book, you will learn why certain styles, details, colors, and other design elements work for you and what is most appropriate for your figure type.

When you have taken stock of your present wardrobe you will have a record that will help you decide what new clothing and accessories you need to sew or purchase. As you become more fashion-conscious, your records should include:

1. An itemized list of your present wardrobe with a short description of each item. For example, navy blue skimmer with drawstring neck, long raglan sleeves, self-fabric belt; denim jeans with straight legs; yellow, long-sleeved T-shirt.

2. A list of colors you feel are complementary with examples of fabric swatches, if possible. Use chapter 4 on color as a guide when you experiment with new color combinations in your wardrobe. Discard anything that is not becoming.

3. A list of the styles of clothes that you feel are figure-flattering and comfortable. For example, lime-green pantsuit (shirt-style jacket, elasticized waistband pants with straight legs, tailored, green print shirt); princess-style dress with wing collar and puffed sleeves; shirtdress with fitted bodice, slightly-fitted A-line skirt.

4. A list of all shoes, bags, boots, hats, scarves, jewelry. Note which are your favorite accessories and ask these questions: Is it flattering and fashionable? Is it just utilitarian? What does it do for the total fashion image when worn with an appropriate outfit?

5. A list of the cosmetics for face, eyes, and lips that help give you a healthy glow. Include your best hair color, too.

6. A list of items to be discarded. Discard every item that does not enhance your new fashion outlook. It must go! It is better to have a few basic pieces that will complement your figure than to have a closet full of unflattering, poorly-fitting, inappropriate clothes.

Now you are ready for this book. Understanding how the shape and proportions of your body influence clothing allows you to highlight your best features and play down the flaws.

Fashion lines of a garment—hems, seamlines, sleeves, necklines—and other fashion details can be used to your advantage, while keeping your outfit balanced and in proportion to your figure. Basic dress silhouettes used by every designer will be presented as they relate to the ample body.

Developing the ability to select the most flattering pattern styles and then following through with appropriate fabric in a becoming color will result in a totally attractive outfit. Color is an area of fashion that is especially important for the woman with a fully-formed figure. Get out of that black, navy, or dark brown syndrome and learn how to select colors that are most becoming and also have excitement.

You will find out how to get additional use from your patterns by easily varying your favorite styles.

Sewing tips will include many fashion details to flatter your particular figure.

The last part of the book deals with accessories and alterations for ready-to-wear. Accessories are very important parts of a large woman's wardrobe, as they can be used to balance the carefully sewn garments on your figure. Alterations may be essential when you choose to purchase some of your fashions, and the examples given are fairly simple to do.

Sewing Big will help you create a dynamic fashion image regardless of your weight or height. It will help you realize your goal—to be well-dressed at all times.

1

Your Figure...
Just As It Is!

When you do not have the foggiest idea of where to start raising your fashion-consciousness, it only seems logical to begin with the most important ingredient—your figure, devoid of all trappings. Understanding the shape of your body will not only make you aware of your best (and worst) features, but will give you the foundation on which to build a totally figure-flattering wardrobe.

The fashion guidelines for each figure type will aid you in picking becoming clothes for *every* activity. You may want to make a file card, listing your best styles and fashion features, so you can take it with you when shopping. Such a record will help you make wise selections and put you closer to your goal of being well-dressed.

Getting Started

The easiest way to get started is to read this entire chapter before making any assessments, then go back and closely examine your own body. You will learn about the five basic figure types that represent the body's silhouette: rectangular; full, round hip; large bust; square; and round. Knowing the characteristics of each type will help you understand your figure assets and liabilities.

You may find out that you do not fit precisely into any of the five categories. If you have a rectangular figure with a large bust, for example, you will need to study all the fashions recommended for both figure types and then adapt the styles from each group that will help you maintain the best balance and proportion. Another example is a body with an extra-large bust and large hips. This figure will have almost the same dressing and fitting problems as a square figure. However, you may vary from the five basic figures—knowing your body is certainly the first step toward dressing with flair.

Determining Your Height Category

You can start assembling fashion information on how to dress your particular figure by determining if you are *average*, *short*, or *tall*, without shoes. The pattern companies proportion misses' and women's patterns for the 5'4" to 5'6" body, which is the average height of most American women. Half-size patterns are scaled for short women, 5'2" to 5'4". Ready-to-wear uses almost the same guide. When all three height categories have the same circumference measurements (waist, bust, hips), the shorter women will have an illusion of chubbiness, while the taller women will present a more slender image.

Measure Your Height

Enlist a friend to help you get accurate measurement. Without shoes, stand against a wall with your head erect and your body balanced on both feet. Have your friend push your hair flat and make a mark on the wall (or on a piece of paper taped to the wall behind your head), in a line straight back from the top of your head. Measure the wall between the mark and the floor.

If your height is less than 5'4", you are considered *short*. Any

measurement between 5'4" and 5'6" is considered *average* height. Any woman over 5'6" falls into the *tall* category.

Determining Your Figure Type

A figure analysis is a very personal thing, and the best way to determine your figure type is to put on an exercise suit of a long-sleeved leotard and tights. If you do not own an exercise suit, a long-sleeved tight sweater and panty hose can substitute. This stretchy outfit covers you from neck to toe and will cling to every curve and bulge, making a silhouette that can be honestly evaluated without the distraction of fashion details present in street clothes.

The ample figure comes in many sizes and shapes, and you do not have to weigh 150 to 200 pounds or more to have a figure of uneven proportions. A woman who tips the scales at 110 could have a body that falls into one of the five figure shapes examined later in this chapter.

If you have been sewing for some time, you probably know whether or not your body measurements match, or come close to, the measurements used by pattern companies for determining pattern size. Pattern adjustments and alterations may bring the pattern's measurements in line with your own, but you may not even have thought about your body's silhouette as seen

from the front, side, and back without clothes. No matter where you have figure problems, thick areas or thin areas, they all need to be considered when striving for a well-groomed, fashion-wise look.

Assess your body silhouette as follows:

1. With your exercise suit on, stand in front of a well-lighted full-length mirror. Stand close to the mirror as you examine every figure detail and feature objectively. Then, step back six to ten feet so you can examine your assets and liabilities and their effect on your total silhouette. Form an oval with your thumb and index fingers and look through it (with one eye closed) to get a better perspective of your figure.

2. Examine your body from every angle, including from both sides, front, and back. Note exactly where extra roundness or thickness is on your figure, and if any areas are much smaller in proportion to other areas.

3. Review every curve and feature of your body as you evaluate the five figure types that follow so you will choose the correct silhouette. This is important, because knowing what figure type you are is essential to selecting the most appropriate styles suggested throughout this book for patterns and when purchasing ready-to-wear clothing.

A Six-Step Figure Analysis

Now, while you still have your exercise suit on, it is time to pinpoint your problem areas. Start at the top of your head and work down to your feet. Be honest in your evaluation of what you see. It can only help you to dress to camouflage problem areas. Do not continue to throw away good money on clothes and fabrics because you do not know for sure what looks good on you. Instead, find out all you can about your shape. The truth may not be what you want it to be, but knowing your own body is the first step in accepting it. Use the following chart to check off the appropriate characteristics as you analyze your total physical presentation:

FACING THE FACTS

---

1. Your height:
   - ☐ Average (5′4″ to 5′6″)
   - ☐ Short (5′2″ to 5′4″)
   - ☐ Tall (over 5′6″)

2. Head size, face shape, neck length, and hair suitability.

   Your head is a factor in balancing your silhouette. Measure around your head at the largest spot just below the hairline. An ample figure has a tendency to make your head look smaller.

   HEAD:
   - ☐ Average (20½″ to 23¼″)
   - ☐ Small (up to 20¼″)
   - ☐ Large (over 23½″)

   FACE SHAPE:
   - ☐ Rectangular   ☐ Oval   ☐ Round
   - ☐ Square   ☐ Narrow forehead, wide jaw
   - ☐ Broad forehead, pointed chin

   FACIAL FEATURES:
   - ☐ Prominent   ☐ Subdued

   SKIN:
   - ☐ Pale (white)   ☐ Cream (beige tones)
   - ☐ Sallow (yellow tones)
   - ☐ Olive (green tones)
   - ☐ Ruddy (red tones)
   - ☐ Bronze (copper tones)
   - ☐ Brown (henna tones)
   - ☐ Black/brown (grey tones)

   NECK LENGTH:
   - ☐ Average   ☐ Short   ☐ Long

   Neck circumference:
   - ☐ Average   ☐ Thin   ☐ Thick

   HAIR BODY:
   - ☐ Average   ☐ Thin   ☐ Thick

   Flattering, balancing length?
   - ☐ Yes   ☐ No

   HAIR LENGTH: For larger women, chin to shoulder length hair that frames the face softly are the most becoming. (See Hair Color and Style in chapter 4 for further information.) Does your hair help to make your head appear balanced and in a pleasing proportion with your body?
   - ☐ Yes   ☐ No

3. Pitch of shoulders, bust size, and ribcage proportions:

   SHOULDERS:
   - ☐ Average   ☐ Wide   ☐ Narrow
   - ☐ Sloping

   BUST:
   - ☐ Average   ☐ Small   ☐ Large

   RIB CAGE:
   - ☐ Straight   ☐ Wide near waist
   - ☐ Tapering to waist

4. Waist in relation to bust and hips.

   Ample figures usually have waists that are six to eight inches smaller than the bust and eight to ten inches smaller than the hips.

   WAIST:
   - ☐ Average   ☐ Thin   ☐ Thick

5. Hips, derriere, abdomen, and thighs in relation to bust.

   American women usually have hips two inches larger than their bust measurement.

   HIPS:
   - ☐ Average   ☐ Narrow
   - ☐ Full, round

   DERRIERE:
   - ☐ Average   ☐ Protruding   ☐ Flat

   ABDOMEN:
   - ☐ Average   ☐ Protruding   ☐ Flat

   THIGHS:
   - ☐ Average   ☐ Large   ☐ Slender

6. Length and size of legs in proportion to torso, and size of knees, ankles, and feet.

   TOTAL LEG LENGTH:
   - ☐ Average   ☐ Short   ☐ Long

   HIP TO KNEE:
   - ☐ Average   ☐ Thin   ☐ Heavy

   KNEE TO ANKLE:
   - ☐ Average   ☐ Thin   ☐ Heavy

   KNEES:
   - ☐ Smooth   ☐ Bony   ☐ Large

   ANKLES:
   - ☐ Average   ☐ Thin   ☐ Thick

   FOOT LENGTH:
   - ☐ Average   ☐ Short   ☐ Long

   FOOT WIDTH:
   - ☐ Average   ☐ Narrow   ☐ Wide

Nothing is more important than a personal figure analysis like the one you have just completed. With this analysis and the information that follows, you can now determine what type figure you have: rectangular; full, round hip; large bust; square; or round. Sometimes, you may seem to fit into two categories. If this is the case, use pertinent fashion advice from both applicable categories.

Rectangular Figure

A long rectangular-shaped torso, broad shoulders, straight hips, and most often a larger than average waist that causes the body to look thick in this area (figure 1–1). The side view usually presents the same smooth lines as the front. Many women with rectangular figures have a small, sometimes flat bust, and round, well-proportioned arms and legs.

Average, short, or tall, the rectangular figure has fairly good proportions and can usually wear clothes well because its nicely formed shoulders and gentle curves are in harmonious scale with the rest of the body. If you are tall and have a rectangular figure, wardrobe planning is easy. Model agencies that use large-size models always select women with this figure type.

Dressing a rectangular figure usually presents only one problem: a thick waist. This figure type is the easiest to clothe as long as you do not call attention to this fairly minor flaw.

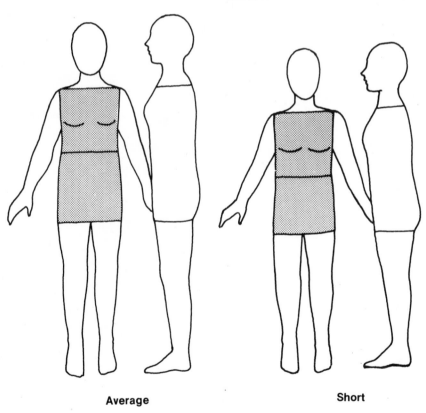
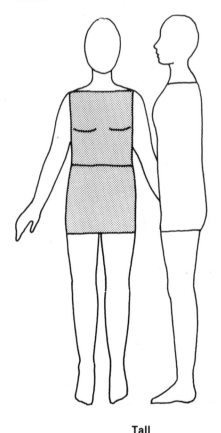

Average

Short

Tall

Figure 1–1: Rectangular Figure

The solution is to de-emphasize the thick waist. Styles such as a dress with an elasticized waist will allow you to fit the bust and hip areas and provide the ease needed for an ample waist. Other dresses and tops without fitted waist seams, or princess and empire styles that do not have exaggerated waist indentations, are some of the best silhouettes to wear. You can wear a belt at the hips, just below the waist, better than any other figure type. Select necklines that will complement your face and neck—V-neck and similar shapes for a round face and short neck, U, round, or bateau for other shapes. Sleeve styles should be fitted or not much fuller than a shirt-type. The length should fall at a flattering spot so it will not add to your waist thickness. The three-quarter or elbow-length sleeve will be the least flattering for you as this length ends near your waist.

The rectangular figure usually looks great in pants and straight skirts. Yours is the only one of the five figure types that can tuck color-coordinated shirts and tops into your pants or skirts. Hip-hugger, dropped-waist style pants and skirts are good choices. They carry the eyes downward, away from the waist.

The following chapters will give you many suggestions for dressing, sewing, and purchasing becoming styles for your particular figure. Be sure to use color to maintain a long, sleek figure without emphasizing your size. Yours is a figure that, with some planning, can be dressed in contrasting and harmonizing colors (see chapter 4).

Full, Round Hip Figure

This figure type, often called pear-shaped, has a narrow top and, usually, a narrow-shouldered torso that continues to the waist area, where it fans out in round hips or large, bulging thighs (figure 1-2). From the side it will reflect the same heavy, lower proportions with a large derriere and sometimes a protruding abdomen. Many full, round hip figures have small, full-cup busts, slightly larger waists, and full, rounded upper arms and legs that taper to normal shapes from elbow to wrist and knee to ankle. Some women with this figure type have thin chests with hips or thighs curving out abruptly below small waists. This shape has been considered beautiful by many artists through the centuries, but whether average, short, or tall, this type of figure is most challenging to clothe in a way that will camouflage the uneven proportions.

Dressing a full, round hip figure can pose a major problem for the fashion-conscious woman. The whole silhouette requires special consideration in order to balance the extremes—the top half must be emphasized with fashion details and accessories to bring it into scale with the lower half, which needs to be minimized.

To overcome the unbalanced look, you need to create a slightly wider appearance above the waist. Use set-in sleeves with smooth or slightly gathered caps to give a wider look at the shoulders but make sure long sleeves taper into minimum fullness at the wrist. You can also wear complementary sleeveless styles with design details that will attract attention and help to bring the upper torso into a becoming scale with the lower portion of your figure. High-waisted and high-fitted dresses, such as empire and princess, or waist-seamed styles with a semifitted look or a little fullness through the waist area will help carry the eye in a vertical line from head to toe. Very full sleeves and wide hems will add to the girth across the hip area, so avoid these. Collars, ruffles, scarves, pockets, and jewelry—as long as these items are not too large—can be used for a heavier influence at the top. Yokes and horizontal seams in the chest and bust area will also add a widening touch. Stay away from tight, wide belts and fitted bodices, as these emphasize the hip girth.

To help minimize the larger hip area, skirts and pants should always have fullness beginning at the widest part of the hips and going straight down or fanning out slightly from there. Fabric falling from the body in this manner will not cup below the hips as you walk and will form a fluid and flattering garment. Although you may yearn for a pencil-thin, straight skirt, with or without side slits, or designer jeans with tapered legs, these styles are not for you. They only accent problem areas, causing you to look broader across the hips. A-line and

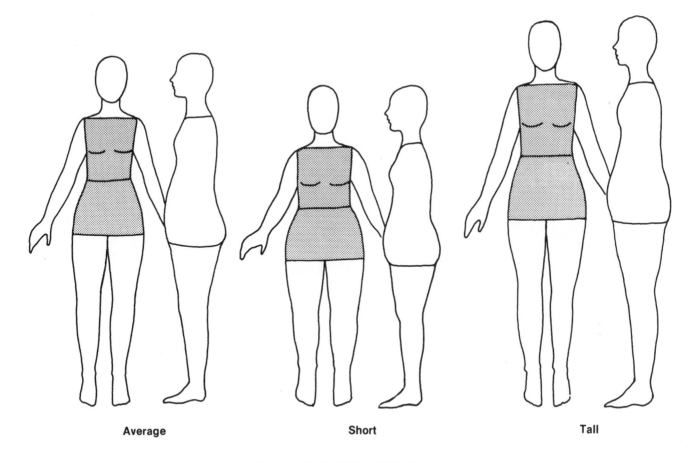

Average

Short

Tall

Figure 1–2: Full, Round Hip Figure

gored skirts are your best choices. Some controlled fullness in the form of gathers or pleats can be used, if the fabric is soft and flowing, and if the excess fabric does not add bulk. Center-front and/or center-back slits, center-front and side-front buttoned closures, and front- or back-wrap skirts will provide a vertical line to camouflage the heavier lower half. Straight-legged pants are the most becoming for the full, round hip figure. Add variety with elasticized waists or unpressed pleats to create softness at the high hip area. Tight-fitting pants will call attention to your hips and may cause the pant legs to collapse and twist, producing the same effect as tapered legs. Stay away from side pockets and horizontal seams in the hip area of a garment. These features will encourage the eye to move from left to right across the figure rather than up and down. As you experiment with the suggestions in the following chapters for full, round hips, you will also learn how to use color to minimize the fuller lower half of your body and to create an illusion of balance.

I have this type of figure, and from time to time, I resent its limitations. Throwing caution to the wind, when straight, fitted side-slit skirts became fashionable, I made this style. Needless to say, the blasted thing never looked right. Every time I caught sight of myself in a store window or mirror, I realized how it accented both my hips and my derriere. The fabric was not ample enough below the widest part of my body for a pleasing look. Not to be without a sexy-looking slit skirt, however, I made an A-line skirt with a center-front slit which was quite flattering. But it had only one slit; so the next time I made one (using the same pattern) I put in both a center-front and center-back slit. I merely added the same extended slit facing to the center-back seam that was given for the front.

You will find simple waist and hip alterations for your figure in chapter 6. If the lack of proportion is very pronounced, it is better to purchase two patterns in order to fit both halves of your figure, making fitting much easier. You will also find the three-size patterns most convenient. With a little thought, you can add variety to your favorite patterns by using details such as gathers, pleats, or different necklines and sleeves.

Large-Bust Figure

This figure has average to broad shoulders and straight, narrow hips. The large heavy breasts may appear to extend from the shoulders to several inches above the waist and protrude outward five or more inches. Older women may have a bust that lies near the waist. The upper arms may be thick, tapering to well-formed lower arms, and the legs are usually thin and shapely (figure 1–3). The side view will show a straight, unfleshy back and buttocks, with full, rounded curves above the waist. The sides (and front) of the hips are without fleshy curves.

This is the most cumbersome of all the figure types. Some women actually feel top-heavy as they walk and have a tendency to stumble.

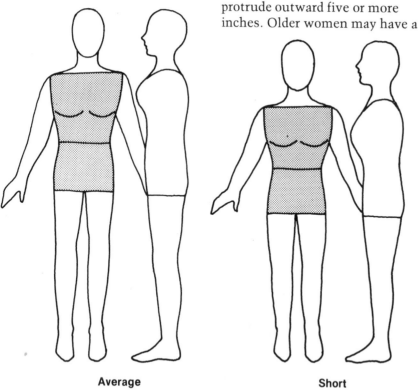

Average

Short

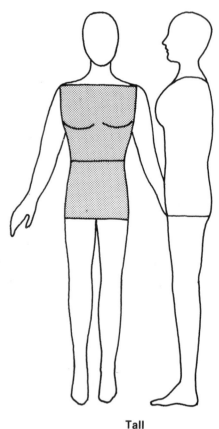

Tall

Figure 1–3: Large-Bust Figure

Dressing a large-bust figure creates fitting and balance problems due to the disproportion of the top in relation to the lower portion—the top portion needs to be scaled down optically and the lower half must be balanced with great care so the total silhouette is visually pleasing.

Dressing a top-heavy figure requires fashion savvy. While some women consider a large bust an asset, most women with an oversized bosom, regardless of their height, find it difficult to dress conservatively without looking matronly.

Determining the best approach requires some careful planning. The bust area needs to be de-emphasized, and a slightly wider or fuller line must be created below the waist to bring the two areas into balance. It is wise to start with a well-built, long-line bra with sturdy straps that will support the weight of your bust. This will give you a firm, well-shaped bust area that will be easier to minimize. Fitted, set-in, raglan and dolman sleeves, and some conservative sleeveless styles, will flatter without adding top-heavy details. Stay away from puffed, gathered, or cap sleeves in any length, as they will add girth to the top. The same is true of short sleeves in any style that end near the fullest part of the bust. Choose a V-, scoop, or U-neck that suggests a vertical area above the bust. Ignore a high cleavage. Many large busts seem to start high on the shoulders and the separation is also high. It is

better to strive for a smooth, flattering neckline and bust area than to select only high necklines that are not always the most flattering.

Fabric over the fullest part of the bust area should drape loosely, being neither too tight nor so full that you have extra fabric folds adding more bulk. Never wear ruffles or large, wide trims over the bust. The ribcage area between the bust and waist should not be emphasized with wide belts or be tightly fitted.

To help counterbalance the heavier top and smaller lower half of this silhouette, skirts and pants should always have a little fullness. Choose skirts and dresses that have skirts with details such as gathers, pleats, and pockets. This will make narrow hips appear to be in a more pleasing proportion to the bust and help minimize the top. Full, A-line, gored, and pleated styles for skirts give a swish to the hem edge that carries the eye downward.

Straight-legged pants are your wisest choice. Styles with pleats and side pockets creating a little fullness are more flattering than skin-tight pants that will only accentuate your larger top.

Pick dresses with waist or hip seams that are easy to adjust and fit. Bodices such as blouson, shirt, or other styles with gathers at the waist or hip seams, will create a softer look without calling attention to the bust. One-piece semi-fitted or slightly-fitted dresses that do not have a waist seam seldom give a pleasing look, as they tend to collapse below the bust in an unattractive manner. Button-front closures

will add a lengthening vertical line down the center of the bust. Choose jewelry and accessories with care, as you want to use these interests to de-emphasize. Keep these items small and color coordinated.

Tops, overblouses, and jackets should be a longer length and should not be tucked into your skirt or pants. Short and tucked-in styles will only serve to accent the bust. Those top garments without a waist seam will need the help of a loose, narrow belt to hold the excess fabric in a pleasing manner over the hips. Arrange the fullness so that it doesn't collapse unattractively below the bosom.

You will find an easy, large-bust pattern alteration in chapter 6. If the lack of balance is very pronounced, it is easier to purchase two patterns and join them at the waist. You can vary and add a new look to your most flattering patterns by substituting some of the fashion details suggested in chapters 6 and 7.

Square Figure

This figure has a thick, wide, short torso with broad shoulders, wide hips, and usually long legs. The center-back measurement from the base of the neck to the natural waist is quite short, with almost no visible waist indentation. In most cases, the bust is small or flat. Big, upper arms and legs taper to thick lower arms and calves with thick ankles (figure 1–4). The side view reflects the same square torso.

If you are tall, your height will have some influence on your silhouette, but many of you may still feel limited when trying to choose a flattering wardrobe. However, a better understanding of your figure will help you find ways to add wardrobe variety and overcome limitations.

Dressing a square figure presents several problems that must be considered—the wide, stocky torso, the thick waist, and a shorter-than-average upper body above the waist.

The solution is to emphasize the vertical. Straight side seams will work for your figure, giving a straight, longer look to the garment silhouette. Empire styles and dresses with high waist seams will follow the contours of your body and create an elongated skirt line that camouflages stockiness. An elasticized casing placed above or at your waistline will give the same elongated effect and provide the ease you need in the waist area. Garments should have enough ease in the bust and hip areas to allow the fabric to drape smoothly over your body and camouflage the waist.

Center-front details such as panels, buttoned closures, and trims give a narrowing vertical line. Straight, slightly full styles are best for your figure. Use V-necklines, long necklaces, scarves, and other accessories that will give a lengthening touch to the center of your garment. Try not to clutter gar-ments with oversized collars, ruffles, or too much trim. Sleeves should be narrow and with a minimum of fullness so they will not add to the illusion of girth.

Separate skirts and pants with straight lines will be your best choice. But due to your short waist length, tops and blouses should not be worn tucked in as they will simply call attention to the waist. Wear long tops, overblouses, and jackets, as your long legs will give an attractive *leggy* look to those types of outfits. Loosely belt appropriate styles at the high hip level—just below your waist—for a pleasing look.

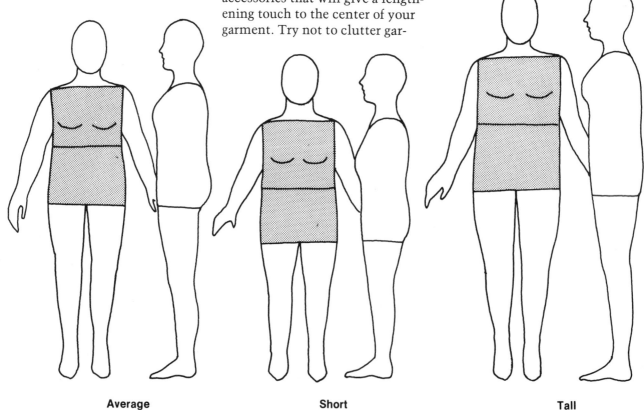

Average   **Short**   **Tall**

Figure 1–4: Square Figure

You may have difficulty buying flattering ready-to-wear clothes, so sewing may be the most practical and economical answer to your needs for a diversified wardrobe. In later chapters, you will find many sewing ideas that are appropriate for your figure type.

Round Figure

This figure type usually has a stocky, round torso with practically no waistline indentation, and wide upper hips that taper to the pelvis. The shoulders are narrow, sometimes sloping. The bust is low and full; big, round upper arms and legs taper below elbows and knees to almost average wrists and ankles (figure 1–5). The side view is rounded in almost the same way as seen from the front and back. Choosing a flattering wardrobe for this figure type requires planning in order to have a varied selection.

Dressing a round figure presents two problems—narrow shoulders and a rounded, almost shapeless torso. None of the body features seem to be especially prominent.

The fashion solution is to create a feeling of balance and proportion that is in scale with your figure and will create an eye-pleasing image. The taller you are, the easier it will be to give some additional length to create a stronger vertical sense.

Average, short, or tall, you should strive for sleek garment lines that will not overwhelm your figure with excess fabric. Avoid tent dresses and caftans with full, dolman sleeves or full, gathered set-in sleeves.

An A-line garment is your most flattering dress silhouette as it follows, without emphasizing, the natural contours of a round figure. Princess, empire, and high-waisted semifitted styles will not accent the problems and are good styles for you.

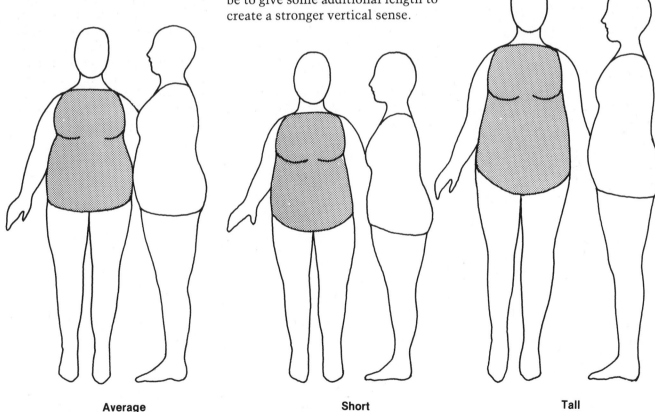

Average　　　　**Short**　　　　**Tall**

Figure 1–5: Round Figure

One-piece dresses with center-front interest are the most flattering: buttoned closures, panels, trims, and ruffles will give a narrowing vertical line that will minimize your girth. Some styles with elasticized casings or belts tied under the bust emulating an empire style are good. Use necklines, jewelry, and accessories that will add a lengthening touch to the center of the garment. Avoid oversized collars, ruffles, accessories, and jewelry that add to the roundness of your silhouette.

To balance the top, use set-in sleeves with smooth or slightly gathered caps to give a wider look at the shoulders. You might try shoulder pads in some of your garments. Keep the sleeve fullness to a minimum, as extra fullness adds girth. Yokes and horizontal seams can give a subdued horizontal effect above the bust, but avoid any contrasting fabric or trim used horizontally. These cause the eye to go

from left to right, giving an illusion of a wider figure.

Garment fullness over the hips should always start at the widest or thickest part of the body. Fabric draping from this area will help create a fluid, flowing garment. Straight side seams are not recommended for this shape as they cause cupping under the hips, outlining the body. The fabric seems to twist and grab at the body instead of swaying gracefully with movement. Instead, choose garments with side seams that gracefully flare.

When wearing separate skirts and pants, the fullness should also begin at the widest part of the hips, so the garment will not cup below the hips, causing an unpleasing line. Select smooth, unadorned elasticized waistband styles that will allow the garment to fit your waist comfortably while having enough fullness over the hips. A-line and gored skirt styles and straight-legged pants work best for your figure.

Skin-tight pants will cause the fabric over your legs to twist and collapse, unattractively accenting the legs in the same manner as tapered pants.

Tops, overblouses, and jackets should be pelvis length, and tops and blouses should not be tucked into your pants or skirt. All of your clothes should be loosely fitted, but not voluminous. Overly full garments will only add to your girth, while closely-fitted ones will accent it.

Sewing may be the most practical way to have a sensationally flattering wardrobe, as there is likely to be little variety in ready-to-wear. Every aspect of sewing covered in this book will help you sew complementary garments. Add fashion details to your favorite silhouette pattern in the form of soft pleats instead of gathers, buttoned closures, necklines with ties, and several sleeve variations. Your imagination can overcome the limitations.

2

Fashion Details

Twice a year the haute couture designers in this country and Europe introduce new styles that set the pace for the ready-to-wear and pattern industries. The styles are often quite innovative, sometimes even too extreme for the work-a-day life of many women. But the designers always include some classic styles that are appropriate for nearly every life-style. In most cases, many of these classic styles will work for you.

You can pick up fashion tips from magazines, newspapers, TV, films, and store displays. When you see a style you like on another woman, make a mental note of that, too. Look for designs that can be adapted to complement your larger figure. Let your clothes express your personality. Find a natural, comfortable look that will fit the way you live.

A flattering ensemble is one that has the right color, lines, silhouette, fabric, and accessories—all selected to meet the demands of the occasion, whether at home, work, sports events, entertaining, out-on-the-town, on vacation, or traveling. In addition, the clothes should fit your body well. Analyze each category— sportswear, day and evening wear— as it pertains to your individual needs.

Design Lines

Look at pictures in newspapers and magazines of haute couture and you will see that what makes these garments special is the creative use of seams and sometimes hems. These are called design lines. Yokes, necklines, shoulder placement, skirt length, and sleeve fullness are some of the dominant garment areas made interesting by the creative use of design lines. Many of these high-fashion styles can be made to work for you.

Some design lines formed by seams are needed for body shaping; others are design lines that add detail and interest to the silhouette. Lines on garments can do strange things when you look at them. *Vertical* lines, for example, make your eyes start at the top and move downward. *Horizontal* lines make your eyes move from left to right. When a garment has lines in both directions, your eyes automatically focus on the horizontal before going to the vertical lines. Other lines, such as *curved* or *diagonal*, may be used effectively as well.

Each garment should be *balanced* on your figure. Balance is created by the *proportions* of your garment, where the design lines fall on your particular body. For example, if you are fairly short and have full, round hips, a balanced outfit for you would be a long, loosely-fitted overblouse and an A-line skirt. The overblouse has long vertical lines that counter the roundness of your hips, and the A-line skirt smoothly continues the vertical lines down over your hips. The length of the overblouse also makes the top of your body look longer, creating an outfit whose design lines bring an out-of-proportion body into proportion. If you find it hard at first to understand what design lines can do, look again at some high-fashion magazines. Compare styles. Some will be loose and flowing, some geometric, others asymmetrical or layered. You should soon see how the design lines make the garments differ, creating a unique look for each one.

Vertical Lines

A seam down the center of a garment (figure 2–1) is considered the most flattering design line for full-figured women, as it gives the illusion of a taller, more slender body (1). The same effect can be achieved with a zippered front or front-buttoned closure.

Two or more vertical seams have a tendency to shorten the design lines, but they still have slenderizing qualities (2). A princess dress with two side-front seams or a dress with a contrasting front panel is a favorite used by many designers. *All five figure types* should emphasize vertical lines to create a long, sleekly balanced look.

Horizontal Lines

Seams or fashion details horizontally placed tend to emphasize width (figure 2–2) when placed on the body at an inappropriate spot.

Figure 2–2: Horizontal lines should be used for balance to help keep every outfit in a pleasing scale.

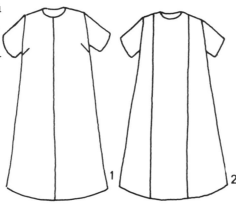

Figure 2–1: Vertical lines give a longer, sleeker look to every costume.

You can, however, use horizontal design lines to your advantage to make a narrow top look wider (1), but this line should not be used by the large-bust figure. It is a great help for a woman who has a narrow top with full, round hips when horizontal yokes or seams fall near the bustline. The lines will carry the eye across the top part of the body and make it seem to be wider, more in proportion with the heavier lower part. Bands, braid, piping, or other types of trim will have the same effect when placed horizontally near the bust. For a rectangular figure, add interest to the lower edge of a dress and retain a fitted or semifitted silhouette (2). Use a pleated or gathered flounce, placing the seam low enough to maintain a well-proportioned garment. The large-bust figure may use a fitted skirt with a hip yoke or seam. Square and round figures may use narrow trim at the hemline in the form of ruffles, bands, and braid if the color is the same as the garment color.

Diagonal Lines

A deep diagonal seamline will give a modified illusion of height (figure 2–3) as it moves from the left shoulder to the right side of the hem edge (1), or vice versa. When using this line, be sure to make the dress in one color and use a semi-fitted or slightly-fitted silhouette. Two colors will make most large women look short and squat.

Two diagonal seamlines that meet at the center and include a high, round neckline in a semi-fitted or slightly-fitted silhouette can also be slenderizing (2). A one-color garment is quite appealing, but a dress with a contrasting panel will add a little dash to an understated wardrobe for *all five figure types*.

Curved Lines

Select a curved seaming detail to emphasize your body curves (figure 2–4), continuing downward to the hemline to give the illusion of a sleeker figure (1). This style of princess dress uses seams instead of bust darts, to give shape, and may have a fairly straight skirt or be quite full when flare is added to each panel. Princess styles can be flattering to just about *any figure*, with the exception of women with a large bust; these figures need a modified version with a waist or high hip seam.

Figure 2–4: Curved lines may be used to add figure-flattering fashion details to any garment.

Curves moving upward will also add slimming details (2). This is a good style for the rectangular figure, but the full, round hip figure may find this line inappropriate, as it

could draw attention to her widest point.

Garment Balance and Proportion

Each garment you see in a store window, on the pages of a pattern catalog or fashion magazine, or on a hanger on a store rack, has balance and proportion sewn into the design. But how many times have you tried on a beautiful dress only to discover that it did nothing for you because of your own body proportions? No matter what your size, not every style will be right for you. Few women have the standard body measurements used by manufacturers and pattern companies. By now I am sure you know exactly how much and where your measurements differ from those used for patterns and ready-to-wear. As you become aware of your own body, you will be able to turn your fashion image from average to outstanding, even when dressed for a weekend at the beach.

Balance and proportion tie all of the elements of good design together. For example, look at the same style two-piece dress on a tall woman and a short woman, flattering to both (figure 2–5). The cowl neckline *balances* the hip-length hem of the top, avoiding a bottom-heavy look. But the taller woman needs a higher horizontal line (formed by the hem of the top) than is required by the shorter woman to keep the dress in *correct proportion* to her figure. Each outfit you wear should be evaluated for these two characteristics.

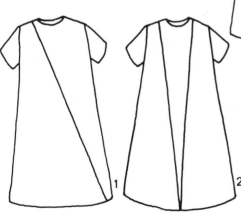

Figure 2–3: Diagonal lines add a graceful touch that helps give an elongated look.

Figure 2–5: Tall or short, the same style is appropriate for both, when the design lines are adapted to the woman's height.

Balance

The focal point of a garment is used for balance—to bring one part of the body, top or bottom into scale with the other part. It may be a double row of buttons on a jacket or coat, a pleated or gathered skirt, a front-buttoned bodice, a contrasting center-front panel, a side-front drape or asymmetrical seaming, or just about anything that makes the body look evenly formed, top and bottom.

Figures that are not in perfect proportion need a little more thought to help create a balanced look. A full, round hip or round figure should wear garments with set-in, plain, or slightly full sleeves and may use pockets, collars, and other fashion details on the top half of an outfit to bring it into scale with the lower half of the body. Garments smoothly draped over the hips, allowing the fabric to flow down and out and away from the widest part will help to add symmetry to these two figure types.

The woman with a large bust will look best in simple bodice fronts that flow smoothly over the top. Keep all neckline treatments flat and unadorned. Softly gathered or pleated skirts may also be used to help strike a good balance between the top and bottom half of the garment. Rectangular and square figures do not have a top-bottom balance problem like the other figure types, but should avoid outfits that abruptly divide the body in half at the middle.

Proportion

Seamlines and hem edges form the horizontal lines that divide sections of a garment or ensemble. These lines can make you look taller and slimmer or shorter and squatter. Moving down the silhouette, it is more interesting and pleasing to the eye if the horizontal lines—neckline, waist, and hem—are not equidistant. The waist seam may move up or down on the body to create different proportions, to lengthen or shorten the torso. A hem of a jacket or top may fall anywhere in the hip area that will not over-emphasize the girth. Hip seamlines and seams over the bust as well as trims in these areas (even topstitching) may make a figure seem broader and shorter.

Horizontal design lines must be in scale with each other from the shoulders to the hem of a dress, skirt, or pants. This does not mean that all horizontal lines must be the same width, but that they make each section of the body look like it is in proportion to the other section, top to bottom.

The large-bust figure should make sure that short sleeves do not end at the fullest part of the bust, or they will give the illusion of an even broader top and shorter body, because they create a horizontal line across the top of the body. The figure with full, round hips or a round shape should not use side pockets or seams that carry the eye across the widest part of the hips. The rectangular or square figure should stay away from padded and extended shoulders, as they will carry the eye across this part of the body, making it seem broader. *All figure types* should select sleeves that are fairly narrow and loosely-fitted or only slightly full. Variations of these types will not put a lot of excess fabric on an already ample figure. Short, puffed, bell, or full, gathered sleeves may create a broadening effect.

When hem lengths are raised or lowered by fashion designers, many women adjust the lengths of their hems. Some garments will retain their proportion, but for others proportion will be disturbed and the garment will no longer have the pleasing overall effect that it first had. Experiment with your wardrobe, thinking about proportion, and take a long look at yourself in a full-length mirror. Those outfits that seem to be all wrong can often be corrected by simply raising or lowering a hemline. CAUTION: A skirt overly long will make a large woman seem dowdy, and a skirt overly short will make her look ridiculous. Keep these things in mind when you are pinning up a hem.

Basic Dress Styles

The basic silhouettes used to create dress pattern styles are quite easy to recognize. The following illustrations are meant to give you a general idea of those that will complement a large woman. In pattern catalogs you will find many interpretations of basic silhouettes. Some may have a fuller hem circumference than others, a looser fit, or may be a combination of a fitted and loosely fitted silhouette, such as a shirtdress with a fitted bodice and a gathered skirt, or a dress with a slightly-fitted blouson bodice and a straight, fitted skirt.

The dresses here are separated into five categories to give you an idea of how the style lines will change as the garment becomes fuller. (See Understanding the Pattern in chapter 3, if you are not familiar with the terms *wearing ease* and *style ease*.)

Fitted Dresses

These silhouettes (figure 2–6) fit at the bust and hips and in most cases at the waist. The large woman must select this silhouette with great care. You will need every bit of style ease to retain the smooth, sleek fit. Be sure to make proper adjustments needed to bring the pattern in line with your figure.

The shirtdress shown is fitted at the bust and hips with a suggestion of a waist fit (1). This style has a slenderizing, vertical line created by the buttoned-front closure. For the rectangular figure this is a perfect silhouette. The full, round hip, square, and round figures will need the addition of a slight A-line shape so that the garment will drape gracefully. The large-bust figure needs a waist seam so the bodice can be well fitted.

The Sheath dress is fitted at the bust, waist, and hips (2), and is best avoided by large women. Rectangular, square, and round figures usually do not find this style flattering, as they rarely have a pronounced waistline. This style is not particularly becoming to the full, round hip, or large-bust figures either, as it may profile the lack of balance between the top half and lower half of the body.

Raised-Waistline dresses will fit at the bust, hips, and two or three inches above the natural waistline. This is sometimes referred to as a *high* fit (3). With or without a raised-waist seam or band, there is a variation for everyone. The rectangular and square figures will be able to wear the straight, side-seam skirt shown, but the round, and full, round hip figures will need an A-shape. The large-bust woman should add a slightly gathered skirt for balance and always wear a style with a waist seam.

Figure 2–6: Fitted Dresses

Semifitted Dresses

This group has a little more circumference over the bust, waist, and hips, allowing the dress to skim over the body, barely touching these three body points (figure 2–7). Do not make the mistake of so many women with ample figures—they use the extra style-circumference to handle the extra girth instead of making the pattern adjustments needed for circumference and still retain the loose, skimming effect. A smooth, fluid flow of fabric will be more flattering than a tight, misshapen garment.

The Princess style has gore shaping that may run from bust to hem or shoulder seam to hem (1). Women with rectangular bodies, narrow top with full, round hip shapes, as well as square and round figures, will find this style flattering when it skims the body gracefully. But the woman with a large bust should not wear a dress without a waist seam,

as it will collapse below the bust and hang in an unattractive way.

Lowered Waistline dresses will have a seam that falls anywhere from two to seven inches below the natural waist. This style is sometimes described as a *hip fit* (2). The woman with a rectangular figure or a large bust with narrow hips will find this style quite adaptable and complementary, with a balancing horizontal line formed by the hip seam. Square, round, and full, round hip figures should stay away from this style, as it will lead the eye across the broadest portion of the body.

The Empire dress has a seaming detail that starts about three to six inches above the waist across the back and continues upward slightly and curves under the bust, usually ending in a point at the center front (3). This style is flattering to *all*

figure types except large bust. In the case of the large-bust figure, it is almost impossible to fit the bodice and skirt without distorting the skirt front. A modified empire bodice—one with a loose-fitting seam under the bust and with a slightly gathered skirt—may be balanced and in proportion on a tall woman with a large bust.

Slightly-Fitted Dresses

In this classification, the dress fits the neck, shoulder, and armhole areas and has a moderate amount of fullness over the bust, waist, and hips (figure 2–8). Even though there is a lot of extra fabric, make all the pattern adjustments you would normally need for a more fitted garment. Otherwise, the lines of the dress will be distorted and could, for example, emphasize just what you want to camouflage. Be sure there will be enough fabric to drape gracefully from the bust in a pleasing manner.

A Shift with almost straight side seamlines will hang freely over the body from a yoke with gathers, or have darts, tucks, shirring, or other shaping detail to give the fullness needed over the hips (1). Rectangular and square figures look great in dresses that hang in a straight line from the underarm. The straight sides are not flattering for the round and full, round hip figures, as the skirt area tends to accent the broadness of their bodies. This style usually collapses below the bust in an unattractive manner on a large-bust figure.

Figure 2–7: Semifitted Dresses

Figure 2–8: Slightly-fitted Dresses

An A-line silhouette is so called because it hangs freely from the bust, and the side seams flare out so the dress takes on an A shape (2). This style may be worn by *all five figure types*. Be sure the fabric drapes fluidly but does not cling, accenting bulges.

A Skimmer style may have a center-front and a center-back panel as well as side seams to give more shaping plus flare at the hemline. It may have a cowl neckline, yoke, band, or other fashion detail, as well as center-front and center-back seams to give an unrestrained fit (3). Every woman should have at least one skimmer in her wardrobe, with or without sleeves. Its vertical lines create the illusion of height, as does the smooth, slight fit. The classic soft denim jumper or a white sundress in the skimmer silhouette, with gored center-front, back, and side seams, are favorites of every woman, young or old.

Loosely-Fitted Dresses

These styles are often called tent dresses because of their fullness. Such dresses have a smooth fit around the neck, shoulders, and usually the armholes (figure 2–9). Choose styles that will fall gracefully over the body. Do not use an extra-full tent dress to hide behind, or you may look like a walking mound of fabric. Full, gathered sleeves or other caftan-style sleeves with full, wide, hem circumferences may put so much fabric at the top that you will be overwhelmed at both the shoulders and hips.

This silhouette begins with bands, drawstrings, narrow, round yokes, or other fashion details that hug the neck and shoulder area. Softly gathered fabric can be cut into gores, creating a full sweep at the hem (1). There may be a yoke that ends at the bustline, and almost straight side seams. The key factor will be fabric selection. This style dress should be made in soft, thin fabrics (2) so it flows over the body and drapes gracefully. *All five figure types* will find this style of dress suitable. The large-bust figure, however, may need a slightly shorter yoke for a loosely-fitted dress with straight side seams, so the gathers start above the bustline and do not give a strong horizontal line at the broadest part of the body.

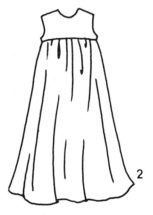

Figure 2–9: Loosely-fitted Dresses

Sleeveless Dresses and Sundresses

The next time summer or a special occasion rolls around, consider something in a sleeveless, strapless, or sundress style (figure 2–10). As a matter of fact, the ample figure looks much better in these styles than do thin, bony figures. You can be sure a strapless dress will be a sensational feature for a dress-up occasion when combined with a well-designed strapless bra that will support the weight of the breasts. The plump woman has smooth lines that extend from the shoulders into the arms in a pleasing manner, and the arms usually enlarge in the same proportions as the body.

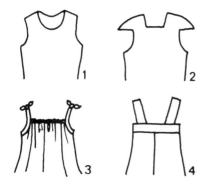

Figure 2–10: Flattering sleeveless and sundress styles for an ample figure.

Sleeves will not hide the size of your arms. In many cases, short or three-quarter length sleeves end in an unflattering spot that seems to emphasize the arm and body size.

Sleeveless dresses should have armhole edges that fall over the shoulder hinge (1). They should be flattering to *all five figure types*, unless the upper arms are extremely large and out of proportion. Be sure the neckline is becoming to your face shape and complements the bareness of your arms so the whole look is balanced. A narrow-shouldered woman must select a sleeveless dress carefully, avoiding armholes that are cut-away and extend inward toward the neck above the shoulder hinge. This only accents narrow shoulders.

Cap Sleeves or Dropped Shoulder Seams are far more flattering than sleeveless dresses for anyone with very large upper arms. Make certain these styles are loose enough for easy, unrestrained arm movement and end at an attractive spot on the arm (2). These styles are quite becoming and comfortable for *all five figure types* and will help keep body proportions in scale. The broad-shouldered woman may find that the cap sleeve may bind or cause the shoulder area to pull in an unattractive manner.

Sundresses should have the straps positioned on the bodice so the outer edge of the strap falls over the shoulder hinge. Experiment with strap widths until you find the right balance for your shoulder and neck area. Sundress straps should be angled to lie smoothly on the shoulders whether they tie (3), or are straight strips (4). Fit straps carefully so they stay in position when being worn. *All five figure types* can wear appropriate sundresses.

Necklines

These fashion details are a very important part of every garment, and it is wise to consider them carefully. If you do not have a swan's neck, there are ways to make your neck look longer. Stay away from high, rolled cowls and turtleneck collars that touch the chin, as they have a tendency to make your neck look short and your head seem too small for the size of your body. V-shaped, scoop, and U-shaped necklines are your wisest choices for a cut-out style, depending on the shape of your face. This does not mean that you are destined to wear only plain-necked garments. The variations of these three basic shapes are numerous (figure 2–11).

V-Necklines

Many large-sized women consider this neckline the most becoming because of its elongated front opening. It also flatters a round face. It may be plain with a faced edge (1), or it may be decorated with flat braid or band trims, or have other fashion details. The wing collar (2) forms a graceful V-neckline with collar and lapels. The shirt-type, when worn open, forms a becoming V-neckline with a notched collar and lapels (3). The shawl collar (4), with the lapels cut in one with the collar, rolls gracefully along the V-shaped neckline.

Scoop Necklines

These necklines expose more flesh around the neck and shoulder area, which helps to create the illusion of a longer, more slender neck

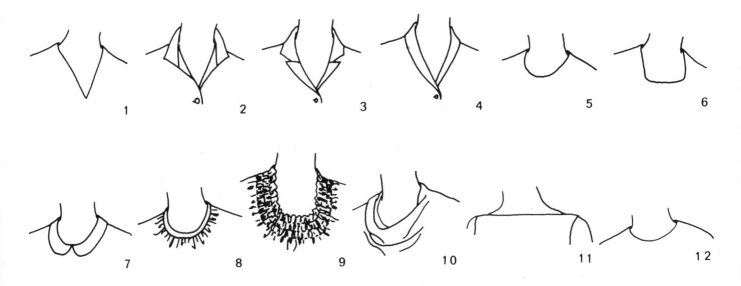

Figure 2–11: Becoming necklines for the large-size woman.

on the ample figure. A scoop neckline (5) forms an attractive round neck opening. It may be lower around the entire neck in the front and back or scooped out in a deep curve at the front, as shown. It will usually flatter most face shapes.

U-Neckline

This neckline has a deeper plunge than the scoop neckline does and is sometimes needed as a balancing influence on the larger figure. However, women with square or round faces may not find this shape flattering. A U-neckline (6) is really a rectangle with rounded corners.

Both the scoop and U-necklines can make the neck look longer for those who need this help. Either shape may be framed with a small collar (7); have a band with gathers for flattering interest (8); or it may be shirred with smocking or elastic (9).

Cowl Necklines

Do not confuse these necklines with a cowl collar, which extends upward along the neck and sometimes touches the chin, making the head seem smaller on a plump body. The cowl neckline (10) has graceful, fluid folds that may drape softly from the base of the neck or form a draped scoop. Cowl necklines are flattering focal points which help balance garments, especially for figures with heavier lower portions.

Bateau Necklines

These straight-line charmers give a plain, uncluttered look. Bateau (the French word for boat) necklines are easy to wear and simple to sew (11). The lines formed across the shoulder and bust area with this neckline create an attractive background for special jewelry. Women with short necks and round or square faces should avoid this style, however, as they may find it unbecoming.

High, Round Necklines

A plain, faced neckline that circles the base of the neck is sometimes called a jewel neckline (12). It creates a simple, unobtrusive line around the neck, allowing the garment to form an elegant foundation for your favorite jewelry. This neckline flatters every facial shape and neck length.

Tops, Overblouses, and Jackets

Any garment worn on the outside over a dress, skirt, or pants must have the lower edge in proportion with the other horizontal lines of your ensemble. There are three lengths that are most flattering to the ample figure, regardless of what type top, overblouse, or jacket is worn. Each garment may be fine in itself, but when combined with another, the proportions may be wrong. Tops, overblouses, and jackets should have the same design lines, be balanced, and in proportion to each other.

Lengths

No matter what type of garment you are wearing, the length must be appropriate for your height and figure. The horizontal line formed by the lower edge of a jacket or skirt should always be higher or lower than the widest part of the body. In this way, the eye is not drawn to the largest area (figure 2–12).

The waist (1) is a favorite length for vests, boleros, sun tops, jackets used to cover a dressy, sleeveless bodice, suit jackets, and sportswear that has an elasticized or drawstring waistband. This length should be suitable for *all five figure types*, if the garment blends with the rest of the outfit with no contrast in color, and has an adequate circumference over the bust and around the waist. (See Wearing Ease and Style Ease, chapter 3.) There is nothing more unattractive than a large woman wearing a vest or jacket that is not ample enough to close properly. This type of badly-fitting clothing only calls attention to the body's girth, because it is obvious the garment is not large enough.

The top of the hip bone (2) has become a favorite sportswear length because it ends two to three inches below the waist. Sweaters, jogging jackets, shirts, and many other tops that have matching ribbing should be suitable for *all five figure types* if they follow the body outline loosely and blend in with the rest of the outfit with no great contrast in color. Overblouses and jackets with straight, hemmed edges will do as well if the edge rests softly on the hips without being tight. A drawstring, elasticized casing, or a narrow belt at the waist is a good fashion feature for this length—especially for the rectangular and large-bust figures.

A garment that ends near the pelvis (3) is a fine length for the curvaceous woman. When the horizontal line ends below the widest part of the body, it leads the eye downward. Worn with pants, a longer garment will give the illusion of height. The swirl of a softly pleated or gathered skirt will add femininity to the long overblouse or jacket. And do not forget those slit skirts, long or street length, which add a sexy touch to any woman's wardrobe.

All five figure types will find the longer top, overblouse, or jacket most flattering. Be sure the hem edge forms a straight, horizontal line around the entire body. Adjust the hem edges, as explained in chapter 9 under the heading Uneven Hemlines, whenever necessary.

Tops

The fashion term *tops* is used for almost any style of separate worn on the top half of the body. Shirt, blouse, tank top, T-shirt, jersey, pullover, sun top, and helenca are some of the common names. But no matter what you call the various styles, be careful. *All five figure types* should avoid tight T-shirts and other tight knit tops, because these garments will emphasize body width. Choose long, slightly- or

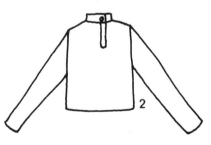
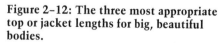

Figure 2–12: The three most appropriate top or jacket lengths for big, beautiful bodies.

loosely-fitted tops, or wear your tops under jackets.

Overblouses

A generic fashion term, it is used to describe any style garment designed to be worn over a skirt or pants. An overblouse may be loose and belted, or may have the same fit as a dress with many variations in style and fullness. Any kind of top not meant to be tucked into a skirt or pants such as a jerkin, tunic, or tabard can be grouped under the general category of overblouse. *All five figure types* can wear suitable, well-fitting overblouses.

Jackets

There are two types of jackets. The first is lightweight or medium weight, worn as part of an ensemble instead of a blouse or top. These jackets fit close to the body and cannot be worn over another garment.

The second type is worn as an addition to a basic outfit. In other words, it may be worn over a dress or blouse and skirt and is made slightly larger than the garments worn under it; so it will slip on and off easily. Jackets require the same attention to a good fit, whether they are used for skiing, as a windbreaker, winter coat, for lounging, or when worn for office use, casual, or dress-up affairs. Jackets are important enough to be considered staples in every woman's wardrobe.

Skirts

There are three general silhouettes for practically all skirts: straight, A-line, and gored. They can

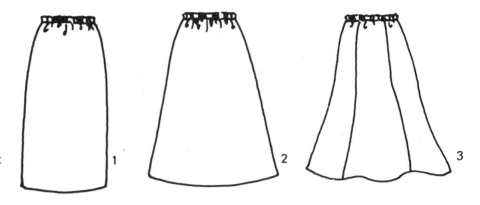

Figure 2–13: The three basic skirt silhouettes.

be worn at any length (figure 2–13). Fashion details such as pleats, yokes, gathers, wrap, buttoned sides or front are simply variations of these three.

NOTE: The sketches show a separate skirt, but these styles are used for dresses as well. When you understand how a skirt should fit and look, it will help you select your most suitable style of dress.

Straight Skirt

Usually fitted at the waist and hips, it hangs over the hips in a straight line to the hem (1). Some may be semifitted or loosely-fitted, with the addition of gathers or pleats, or other design features. All have one feature in common— straight seams and a vertical line from the hips. The woman with a rectangular, large bust, or square figure will be able to wear just about any straight skirt. Those with full, round hips or large thighs, or a round figure should avoid this style, as a fitted, straight skirt has the

tendency to cup below the hip curves, accenting the hips.

A-Line Skirts

This style has side seams that fan outward (2). The addition of buttoned closures, gathers, pleats, and other style features may change the A-line to a semi-fitted or slightly-fitted skirt, but the garment will retain the A-shape at the sides. This skirt is complementary for *all five figure types.*

Gored Skirts

Hugging the waist and the top of the hips, the gored skirt fans out to a fuller silhouette (3). Six or more triangular-shaped panels, called gores, are stitched together to create the shape. Gored skirt patterns are fairly easy to adjust because of all the seams running over the hips. Select any gored skirt that feels good and looks good on your figure, as the vertical lines make this style suitable for *all five figure types.*

Pants

Almost every well-dressed woman has several pairs of pants (figure 2–14) in her wardrobe. Included may be the classic pantsuit that is so convenient for work and traveling, designer jeans, and soft fabric pants for lounging. The larger-size woman, whether of average height, short, or tall, must select pants and their companion garments with care.

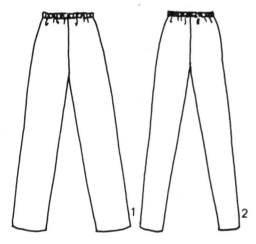

Figure 2–14: Straight-leg or slightly tapered-leg pants are best for most large women.

Many women tend to choose a pair of straight-leg, doubleknit pants that are too tight. They buy for size and not for a good fit. Because the knit fabric will stretch over bulges many women wear pants that merely cover their bodies without enhancing their appearance. When knits are stretched too much over the hips and abdomen, this stress radiates to the pant legs, causing them to twist and collapse, even making the legs shorter. The stretch in knit pants is meant to allow for the stress of action, not to allow you to buy a smaller size. You know from experience that denim pants do not stretch, and you must wear a size large enough to allow you to move and bend. When you must buy a larger waist size to fit your hips, alter the waist as explained in chapter 9.

When pants are topped with a poorly proportioned garment, it only serves to accent a bad fit. As explained in the section on Tops, Overblouses, and Jackets, there are three good lengths for all figure types. At the beginning of this chapter, *design lines* as well as *balance* and *proportion* were defined in relation to fashion. It may be wise to review this in relation to pants. Not many large women should wear blouses tucked into pants, because of figure problems, but a top, overblouse, or jacket that falls at a pleasing length will help draw the eye away from the broadest part of the body. With a little time and effort, complementary, smart-looking pants outfits can be part of every large woman's wardrobe.

Straight-Leg Pants

Many styles of pants have been popular over the years, but the straight-leg styles (1) are the best choice for *all five figure types*. The pants must be large enough to drape smoothly over the hips. The waist should be snug and the legs should hang in a vertical line from the fullest part of the body. The straight legs also give an illusion of added height and tend to hide bulk.

Slightly-Tapered-Leg Pants

This style (2) is quite acceptable for those who have well-shaped legs that are in proportion with your hips, regardless of the figure type. The rectangular and large-bust figures usually have the best legs to show off, while the full, round hip, round, and square figures will need the help of a pelvic-length overblouse or a slightly longer tunic to create a lean and lanky look. The top should be semifitted or slightly-fitted, otherwise the excess fabric of the garment may create a mushroom effect.

Pants Length

No matter which style you wear, straight or tapered legs, make sure the pants hem touches the arch of the foot in the front, with the back ending where the shoe and its heel meet. This way, the length will be appropriate for all heel heights and the ankles will be covered, showing only the shoes. The hem may be slightly longer in back than in front. Large women need this length to keep the feet in proportion to the rest of the body. Too much ankle showing disturbs the overall scale and makes the wearer look short and squat, while pants that are too long collapse and create ugly horizontal wrinkles below the knee.

Fashion Lines by Figure Type

For quick reference, styles are listed according to figure type. Review each style section for complete information.

Rectangular	Full, Round Hip	Square	Round	Large Bust
Shirtdress	Raised-waist with A-shape	A-line shirtdress	A-line shirtdress	Shirtdress with waist seam
Raised-waist dress	Princess dress	Raised-waist dress	Raised-waist with A-shape	Raised-waist dress with gathered skirt
Princess dress	Empire	Princess dress	Princess dress	Lowered-waistline dress
Lowered-waistline dress	A-line dress	Empire dress	Empire dress	A-line dress
Empire dress	Skimmer dress	Straight shift	A-line dress	Skimmer dress
Straight shift	Tent dress	A-line dress	Skimmer dress	Tent dress
A-line dress	Sleeveless dress	Skimmer dress	Tent dress	Sleeveless dress
Skimmer dress	Cap sleeve and drop shoulder dress	Tent dress	Sleeveless dress	Cap sleeve and drop shoulder dress
Tent dress	Sundress	Sleeveless dress	Cap sleeve and drop shoulder dress	Sundress
Sleeveless dress	A-line skirt	Cap sleeve and drop shoulder dress	Sundress	A-line skirt
Cap sleeve and drop shoulder dress	Gored-skirt	Sundress	Straight skirt	Gored skirt
Sundress	Straight-leg pants	Straight skirt	A-line skirt	Straight-leg pants
Straight skirt		A-line skirt	Gored skirt	Tapered-leg pants
A-line skirt		Gored skirt	Straight-leg pants	
Gored skirt		Straight-leg pants		
Straight-leg pants				
Tapered-leg pants				

3

Pattern Selection

The next time you go pattern shopping, look at the pattern catalogs as if almost everything were designed for you. While the largest selection of styles is in misses' sizes (6–20), this does not mean the designs are not appropriate for the large woman (figure 3–1). Notice how the proportions stay nearly the same when extra weight is added to the misses' figure. It just becomes rounder and fuller. Familiarize yourself with the styles that are available for your size, noting silhouettes, sleeves, and necklines. Find the many variations of those same style features that are shown throughout the catalog.

Select a style that will flatter you. If you find a new design in a style that you have never worn and are not sure how it will look on you, find a similar design in ready-to-wear and try it on to see if it is a style you *can* wear. Do not be shy about trying on dresses when you have no intention to buy. It can be fun to do, and it will save you from buying the wrong patterns.

Pattern purchases should be made *after* you have taken proper measurements over well-fitted undergarments. There is nothing less attractive than clothing that is too tight (figure 3–2). Tight clothing emphasizes every bulge (figure 3–3). The opposite is true of clothes that are too loose. If you wear a tent dress or caftan that looks like a shapeless sack, it hides imperfections and best features alike.

Understanding the Pattern

Every pattern has a little extra circumference, built in for movement and comfort, called *wearing ease*. There may be additional fullness or style features in the form of gathers, pleats, tucks, etc., called *style ease*.

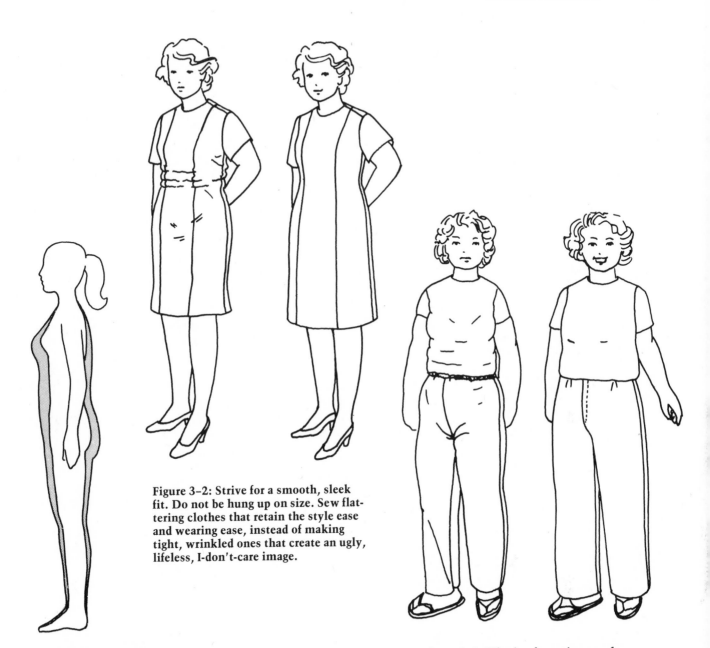

Figure 3–2: Strive for a smooth, sleek fit. Do not be hung up on size. Sew flattering clothes that retain the style ease and wearing ease, instead of making tight, wrinkled ones that create an ugly, lifeless, I-don't-care image.

Figure 3–1: The healthy, ample body that gets sufficient exercise usually has the weight distributed evenly over the entire frame.

Figure 3–3: Whether for action or relaxing, clothes that have adequate style ease and wearing ease are more becoming. Sew an outfit with vertical lines for the illusion of length, such as straight-leg pants and a blousy, waist-length top.

Most pattern envelopes will have a short, descriptive paragraph on the back that gives important information about the style you have selected. *Wearing ease* and *style ease* are very important terms when you are considering how clothes should fit, and how to make them fit. Your pattern style may be described as fitted, semifitted, slightly fitted, or loosely fitted. These are important keys that will take some of the mystery out of the finished product. These terms let you know how the garment should fit, and if the style is one you should consider.

Wearing Ease

The secret to a good-looking garment is understanding how and why patterns fit the way they do. Fitted styles include just the extra room, or wearing ease, needed to sit, bend, stoop, reach, and walk. If clothes were made to your exact measurements you would not be able to move. At different areas of the body, patterns have varying amounts of added width. Usually there is an extra 3 to 3½ inches added at the bust for most size ranges. At the waist, ¾ to 1 inch, in dresses, and ½ to 1 inch in skirts and pants is given. At the fullest part of the hips, 2 to 2¾ inches is allowed. Sleeves have from 1 to 1½ inches at the fullest part of the upper arm. The amounts of wearing ease given here are just for fitted garments—semifitted, slightly-fitted and loosely-fitted clothes all have style ease added to their designs. Also, these figures are for garments made from *woven* fabrics. The patterns for knits compensate for the stretch built into the fabrics. You will see many patterns that indicate they are for certain types of knitted fabrics only. These patterns have less wearing ease added; some of the stretchiness of the knit is used instead. So whenever a pattern says it is for knits only, that is exactly what it means. If the pattern is used for woven fabrics, it will be too tight, even if you have made your usual pattern adjustments.

However, some styles are meant to be tightly fitted in some areas. Sundresses, halter tops, and evening dresses may have exact body measurements around the chest, bust, and rib cage.

Style Ease

This is another factor that you should understand in order to select an appropriate pattern. Designers add fullness in specific body areas to make style variations. This extra circumference built into the design is called style ease, because what it does essentially is change the look of the style, not make it wearable, as does wearing ease. Garments may be made fuller over the bust by loose shaping, gathers, gores, and pleats. These features are usually carried downward over the waist and hips in a pleasing way to make the design appear fluid. Some styles may have a fitted bodice with a semi- or loosely-fitted skirt made with gores, gathers, or pleats. Others will just skim the body, ending with a pleasant A-line or gored silhouette. The sweep of the skirt may be restricted to a skimpy sheath or widened into a full circle, but all patterns are designed with perfect balance and proportion. It will be up to you to maintain the balance and proportion as you adapt the pattern to your needs (figure 3–4).

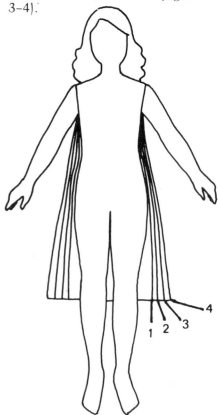

Figure 3–4: Style Ease

Fitted Garments

These garments have only the standard wearing ease allowed for the bust, waist, and hips and usually follow body shape. This type of garment requires the most alterations to get a proper fit. Women with noticeable figure flaws and problems with figure balance will do best to avoid these styles (1).

Semifitted Garments

These garments usually have some style ease over the bust that drapes smoothly to the hem, often nipped in slightly at the waist. Be sure to retain these style lines when making pattern adjustments and alterations. The style lines will be distorted if you try to use up the extra circumference instead of making the needed changes. If your body has fairly balanced proportions, you should be able to wear this type of garment (2).

Slightly-fitted Garments

These garments will have a little more style ease than the semifitted silhouette; from bust to hem, there is barely an indication of the body shape. Be sure to retain the style lines when making pattern adjustments and alterations. You may not need as much additional circumference adjustment as is needed for fitted and semifitted silhouettes. Strive to retain the fluid lines of the style. This type of fit is suitable for most large women (3).

Loosely-fitted Garments

These garments may have considerable style ease, and physical movement suggests there is a body underneath. You may not need to make any circumference alterations or adjustments for these styles. Just make sure the hemline hangs evenly all around the body. Be careful with this style, as too much full-

ness can add bulk rather than camouflage it (4).

And Now It Is You!

Sewing for an ample figure, whether tall, average, or short requires complete honesty. The only way to do this is to find out your exact body measurements. With this information, you will be able to select properly-fitted undergarments that will give you a smooth body. Wearing figure-flattering underthings allows you to get the accurate measurements which will determine your correct pattern size. The end result will be well worth the time spent.

Well-fitted Undergarments

The best seamstress in the world would be hard-pressed to make clothes fit well over poorly-fitted undergarments (figure 3–5). And you know it would be a big mistake to go braless, or wear no undergarments at all. Leave that way of dressing to teenagers and skinny fashion models. Your bra must support the weight of your bust, and the cup must be ample enough for your bust fullness. Many women make the mistake of purchasing a bra that is too big—it rides up in the back over the shoulder blades and allows the bust to point down in front.

If you wear a girdle so tight that you cannot laugh, make sure that it is not so constricting that it forces the flesh upward into the waist and rib-cage area, causing unsightly rolls, or that it cuts into the flesh on

the thighs, creating a bulge below the girdle line.

Panties can cause as many unsightly bulges and ridges as a girdle, if they are too tight. Most women with ample figures have soft flesh,

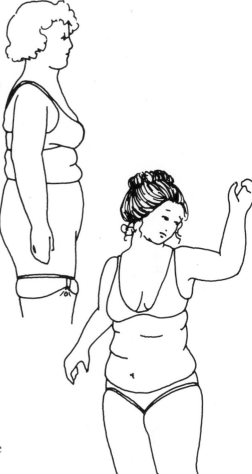

Figure 3–5: Wear properly fitted undergarments. Whether you prefer the firm support of an uplift bra and girdle or a stretch bra and bikini panties, you should avoid undergarments that are too small. They cause fleshy wrinkles and fatty bulges in areas that should have smooth contours.

due to fatty deposits, through the waist, hip, and upper leg areas that will puff out above and below tight panties.

Measuring for Undergarments

Instead of guessing at the size of undergarment you should purchase, have yourself measured at the store, have a friend measure you, or measure yourself in front of a full-length mirror (figure 3–6). Measure over your present underthings, without outer clothing. Hold the tape snug, but not too tight.

HOW TO TAKE MEASUREMENTS

1. Chest: For bra size, measure around your body above the bust and well up under the arms, straight across the back.

2. Bust: For cup size, measure around your body at the fullest part of the bust, straight across the back.

3. Waist: For girdles and half-slips, stand relaxed, your weight balanced evenly on both feet. Measure around your body at the smallest part of your waistline.

4. Hips: For panties and girdles, measure around your body at the fullest part, usually eight to nine inches below the waist. Slide the tape up and down to find the fullest point.

5. Girdle Length: For foundation garments, place the tape at the waist and measure down along the side of your hip to where you want the girdle to end.

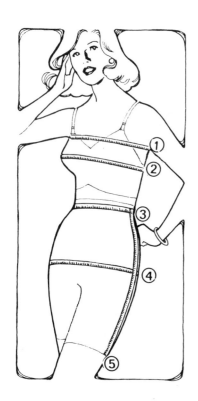

Figure 3–6: Undergarment measuring sketch, reprinted courtesy of Roaman's Mail Order, Inc.

Bra Size: Bra sizes are determined by your chest measurement. When you fall in between sizes, purchase the size nearest your measurement. Bra closures are adjustable for this reason.

To figure out the cup size, use the chart courtesy of Roaman's Mail Order, Inc.. Your cup size is the number of inches your bust measurement exceeds your chest measurement.

ORDER CUP SIZE	B	C	D	DD or E	F
If bust measurement is larger than chest measurement by:	1 to 2 inches.	over 2 and up to 3 inches.	over 3 and up to 4 inches.	4 to 5½ inches.	over 5½ inches.

Panty Size: Panties are purchased in the size nearest your hip measurement.

Full-Slip Size: Full-slips are purchased in the size nearest your bust measurement, not your bra size (chest) measurement.

Half-Slip Size: Half-slips are purchased in the size nearest your waist measurement.

Girdle or Corset Size: Panty girdles, step-in girdles, health belts, and corsets are purchased according to your waist measurement. Choose styles that come in the measurement you need. Most girdles are designed for hips eight to ten inches larger than the waist. If your hips are larger than the stated size for your waist measurement, purchase the next larger size.

Use the following chart, courtesy of Roaman's Mail Order, Inc., to determine the size needed for your slips, girdles, and corsets.

Determine Corselette or Bodysuit Size: Corselettes (bra and girdle combined in one garment) and bodysuit shapers are purchased according to your bra size. If you have a full, round hip figure or a large bust, you should select a long bra and a girdle instead of a corselette, for a smooth, sleek fit.

The subtleties of selecting and wearing the right undergarments are more complex than first appears. Every woman should make a decision to buy comfortable, well-fitting underthings in the correct size to enhance everything she wears.

Measuring for Your Pattern Size

Just as accurate measurements are needed to decide which undergarment size is the best for your figure, some of the same as well as additional accurate measurements are needed to find out which pattern category is the most viable one for you. Put on your properly-fitted undergarments before you start. It is very important that you follow each step as directed. For some measurements, you will need an able assistant, preferably someone who sews (figure 3–7). While some of the measurements seem to be the same as for those needed to buy proper undergarments, they will probably be slightly different when taken again, when you are wearing your new, proper undergarments.

Take your measurements as follows:

1. Stand in front of a mirror to take your measurements so you can be sure the tape measure is parallel to the floor for accurate circumference measurements.

2. Measure over well-fitting undergarments.

3. Make tape measure snug, but not tight enough to make an indentation in your flesh.

4. Mark your waist at the thinnest part with a string.

ORDER WAIST SIZE:	30	32	34	36	38	40	42	44	46	48	50
If hips measure:	38/39	40/41	42/43	44/45	46/47	48/49	50/51	52/53	54/55	56/57	58/59

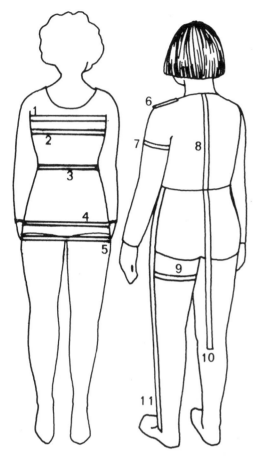

Figure 3–7: Measurements needed for your correct pattern size.

Record the following measurements, making sure you read the tape accurately:

1. High Bust: Place the tape under your arms and above your bust, across the widest part of your back.

2. Full Bust: Place the tape over the fullest part of your bust and straight across the back.

3. Waist: Measure over the string that was tied around your thinnest part.

4. Hip: With the tape straight across the back and front, measure around the body at the fullest part. Slide the tape up and down till you find the widest point. NOTE: The fullest part is usually seven to nine inches below the waist. Mark undergarment with a pin at the tape edge, where the widest point of your hips is, then measure down from your waist to the pin to establish your *hipline.* This measurement is most helpful when adjusting patterns, especially pants.

5. Pelvis: With legs together, place tape around the body at the fullest part at the pelvic area, just at the crotch, and measure.

6. Shoulder Length: Place tape on top of your shoulder and measure from the base of your neck to the end of the shoulder bone.

7. Arm: Place tape around your upper arm at the fullest part, usually just below the armpit. Measure both arms and record the largest measurement.

8. Back (Neck to Waist): Place tape at the center of your back and measure from the prominent back neck bone to your waist string.

9. Thigh: Place tape around your upper leg at the fullest part. Measure both legs and record the largest measurement.

10. Skirt Length: Place tape at the center of your back waist and measure to the spot on your legs where your most flattering skirt hem should end.

11. Pants Length: Place tape at the side of your hip (where the pants side seam would fall). Measure from your waist to just below the ankle bone.

How to Determine Your Pattern Size

Compare your measurements with the standard body measurements on the back of the pattern envelope or on the counter catalog measurement chart, usually in the back of the book.

The pattern industry has established measurements, after years of research, that are the most average of each size (figure 3–8). Misses' and women's sizes are for females 5'5" to 5'6" tall without shoes. Half-size patterns are for women 5'2" to 5'3" without shoes.

As you compare your measurements, it will soon be obvious that you are not a standard body specimen, but a unique, one-of-a-kind woman. It is likely that there is not another person in the world with your exact measurements.

Pattern companies recommend using the pattern size that is nearest to your bust measurement, as it is easier to alter other pattern areas if needed. Recently, the pattern companies have been suggesting that you use the high-bust measurement instead of the full bust when determining your pattern size. Although the high-bust measurement is not a standard body measurement listed on the pattern charts, when there is a difference of two inches or more between the high-bust and full-bust measurements, the high-bust measurement will denote the best pattern size for you.

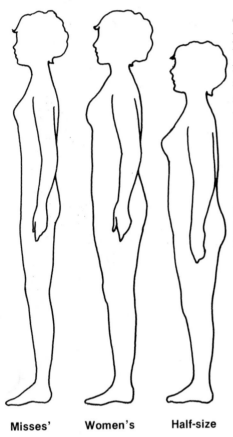

Misses'   Women's   Half-size

Figure 3–8: Pattern size categories.

ences, it may be easier to buy two patterns and combine them at the waist to achieve the best fit. This may seem like an expensive proposition, but the time you save in altering one-half of the pattern to fit your body may be worth the money spent.

Do not be concerned that you may be taller than the half-size patterns allow for, or that you are shorter than stated for women's sizes. Lengthening and shortening patterns are the easiest changes to make.

For a quick reference point, make a comparison chart showing your measurements and those of the pattern size you purchased. The following example shows the standard body measurements printed on the back of the pattern envelope. The appropriate pattern measurements (for a size 20½) are taken by measuring the actual pattern between seam lines. Use the standard body measurements (SBM) given on the envelope, not the actual pattern measurement (PM), wherever possible.

When you are less than an inch over the pattern's measurement for bust, purchase the smaller size.

Some of the pattern companies are featuring patterns that have two or three sizes for each pattern piece on the same pattern. This is a great help to those who have a small bust with large hips, or a large bust with narrow hips. For extreme differ-

COMPARISON CHART

Your Measurements	Pattern Measurements	Adjustment Needed
1. Bust 42½″	43″ (SBM)	−½″ or none
2. Waist 37½″	37½″ (SBM)	none
3. Hip 46¾″	45½″ (SBM)	+ 1¼″
4. Pelvis 47½″	47″ (PM)	+ 2½″ (inc. 2″ wearing ease)
5. Shoulder 5″	5¼″ (PM)	−¼″
6. Arm 16″ (Upper arm)	15⅝″ (PM)	+ 1⅜″ (inc. 1″ wearing ease)
7. Back 18″ (Neck to waist)	16″ (SBM)	+ 2″
8. Thigh 20¾″	20″ (PM)	+ 1¼″ (inc. 1″ wearing ease)
9. Skirt 26″ Length	24¾″ (SBM)	+ 1¼″
10. Pants 41½″ Length	39¾″ (SBM)	+ 1¾″
11. Height 5′7″	5′2″–5′3″	+ 4″

While the chart implies that you might have a lot of pattern changes to make, this is not always the case. If you are making a slightly- or loosely-fitted dress, probably the only changes you would make would be for length. The chart represents what you would have to do to make a *fitted* garment fit. Depending on style, there will be some areas of semifitted and slightly-fitted garments that need alteration, too, but certainly not all of those listed on the chart.

If you are not familiar with all the pattern adjustments and alterations you might need in order to fit your one-of-a-kind figure, now is the time to review these techniques to make sure you will do the necessary changes correctly. Each pattern company now has patterns especially created to solve fitting problems that are well worth the investment of time and money.

Now that you know how to determine your correct pattern size, you are ready to select a style that is appropriate for you.

Pattern Styles for Special Sizes

At this point, you should know your figure type, have a good understanding of design lines used to create different garments, know how to interpret pattern silhouettes and fit characteristics, and know which pattern-size category you should select from, and your pattern size.

This may all seem quite overwhelming as you review it, but if you are serious about dressing with flair and taste, in keeping with your life-style, you must consider *each* aspect of dressing well.

The styles will again be broken down into the five figure types, with several examples in each group; but many styles will be suitable for all figure types, if they are fitted well with the proper pattern adjustments.

Dresses

Dresses are the most flattering garments for the woman with an ample figure. Garments made of one fabric with a minimum of seaming and a pleasing flare at the hemline are the most complementary. You may like a narrow belt or a waist seam—others may prefer a dress that hangs from the shoulders to the hemline, uninterrupted. You can add a matching jacket to most dress styles for a chic outfit that can be worn anywhere.

The major pattern companies' catalogs show more dresses than any other wardrobe item. Look for A-line silhouettes with or without a center-front seam that has a V-neck; slit neckline; draped cowl; narrow neckband with ties; with or without ruffles; a shirt collar; drawstring neckline; a round yoke with band around the neck and down the front; a round yoke with a front slit; and all styles of sleeves in all lengths. Many of the styles will have a top that is a short version of the dress that you can wear as an overblouse with a skirt or pants. Some of these style features will also be shown on dresses with straight side seams.

Most catalogs have three-piece dress, jacket, and skirt ensembles. You will find a lot of loosely-fitted dresses with round and square yokes, drawstring necklines, and narrow-band necklines, usually with raglan sleeves in several lengths and finishes.

Several very flattering princess styles are usually also available. Empire, or high-waist dresses, have many variations in the different pattern catalogs.

Among the many patterns offered by the major companies, you will usually be able to find a suitable style. The whole range of dresses is there, from casual housedress to evening gown. But sometimes the selections for women's and half-sizes seems too limited for your needs. If this is the case, use your creativity. Make the top of a dress into a blouse, or lengthen a sundress into an evening gown. Interchange the sleeves, or collar, of dress patterns to get the style you want. (See chapter 6 for Pattern Changes.)

Tops and Overblouses

These garments add versatility to any wardrobe. As a large woman, you must select yours with extreme care. Top and overblouse patterns have many of the same design line and fit characteristics as dresses; so what looks good on you as a dress style will also work for an overblouse or top. The length of these garments is what you must be cautious about, as you probably will not be wearing them tucked into your skirts or pants. Your figure type will be the deciding factor.

What proves to be in proportion to pants may not look good with a skirt, or vice versa. Generally, a top will not be too loose fitting, so it should end a bit below the waist. An overblouse, since it is looser, in most cases will look best if it ends in the area of the pelvis.

Jackets

Jackets need the same consideration as tops and overblouses. To complement most ample figures, blazers, shirt-jackets, and other jacket styles will look best at a pelvic length. Short styles should rest on the top of the hips or end at the waist. Jackets have most of the same design lines and features as dresses. Once again, a good dress style for you will be a good jacket style. Jackets to be worn over other garments have additional ease built in; so the armholes, shoulders, bust, and hip areas will fit over sweaters and blouses. Jackets shown on the pattern envelope as a cut-off version of a dress are usually only meant to be worn over a dress or lightweight top. Look for jackets with back and side vents, as these are good features for large women. (See how to add vents and a center-back pleat in the Jacket section of chapter 6.)

When making a jacket, be sure it is large enough to fit comfortably over what it is supposed to fit over—bulky blouse, sweater, or top. Jackets should hang freely from the shoulders and fit smoothly around the hips and over the garment worn underneath, and should button easily. Take the same care when fitting jackets without buttons or other closures. Please do not eliminate your usual hip adjustments in the pattern pieces just because the jacket does not button or have a zipper closure in the front, or it will look skimpy and unattractive. The center front edges of these styles should meet when held together with adequate wearing ease allowed, so the jacket drapes gracefully over the hips.

Coats

Coats require the same thought as dresses and jackets. The style and lines must be balanced and in proportion to your height and figure. The few designs shown in the pattern catalogs in women's and half-sizes are usually classic and appropriate for a large woman. Your main consideration will be choosing the right fabric (see chapter 5). You may want to vary a coat design with a center-back pleat, or make a shorter version with side vents. (These details will be explained in chapter 6, Pattern Variations.) Most coats are designed as outerwear to be worn over other clothing. However, if you have selected a pattern which has a coat also shown in a shorter version, as a jacket, you will not be able to wear that coat over the jacket, as both designs are for outerwear only, not for layering.

Pants

These have been a favorite for years. Most of the pants patterns in women's and half-sizes will have fully or partially elasticized waists, and will be meant to wear with overblouses. Your choice of leg style will probably be limited to straight ones, making it necessary for you to vary the leg width. What is most important is the length of the top or overblouse you wear with pants. Experiment with top lengths. In most cases, the top of the hips (a few inches below your waistline), or just below the pelvis, covering the hips to the crotch, are the most flattering lengths. Longer lengths for jackets and shirt-jackets are also flattering with pants.

Skirts

Skirts are avoided by many large women, and this is a mistake, especially if you have trim calves and ankles. There are many skirt types—wrap, elasticized waists, buttoned fronts, etc.—that are very flattering, particularly to the large-hipped figure or one with large thighs. Showing your legs can add to the femininity of your appearance.

Gored and A-line silhouettes are very becoming skirt styles. Front and back kick pleats, or several low pleats can be flattering, too. Steer clear of all-around pleated skirts. Gathers near the sides of the hips can be flattering when used in place of darts or gores, especially if the fabric is soft. To add style details to your favorite A-line skirt, see Gathers, Pleats, Buttoned Front, or Elasticized Waistband in Pattern Variations in chapter 6. To make skirts without a pattern, see chapter 7.

Fashionable Styles for You

Now that you are aware of the great variety of pattern styles available, your next step will be to evaluate these possibilities and see which is right for your figure. The following information is given for each of the five figure types. If you do not fit into one figure category (you have characteristics of more than one figure type) you may find that certain styles selected for each category you have characteristics of will work very well for you.

Rectangular Figures

Nearly every style should flatter your figure except those with a defined, snugly-fitted waistline (figure 3–9). To carry the eye away from a thick waistline, choose dresses with a dropped-waist seam or a two-piece dress with a semifitted overblouse and a straight, or A-line skirt. A slightly-fitted shirtdress with an elasticized waistline treatment and a straight skirt is one style that most other figure types cannot wear, but this will be quite flattering for you. Empire styles, drawstring necklines, and blouson styles are appropriate for the rectangular figure. When selecting a suit, look for a jacket cropped at the top of the hip bone, a skirt with an elasticized waist in a gored, straight, or A-line style, and a blouse with an interesting neckline and any style sleeve to complete a classic, tailored look. Naturally, many of the semifitted, slightly-fitted, or loosely-fitted styles will do your figure justice.

Figure 3–9: Styles that will help de-emphasize a thick waist on a Rectangular Figure.

Full, Round Hip Figures

With a pear-shaped body, you must be keenly aware of balance and proportion (figure 3–10). The narrowness of your shoulders should not be accented by sleeve styles or cut-away sleeveless garments. Set-in sleeves are your best choice. Shorter, cap sleeves are better than some sleeveless designs, and sun or sleeveless dresses and tops should have the edge of the strap or armhole fall over the arm hinge to help create a wider look across the neck and shoulders. To help balance the top portion, use a shoulder treatment with yokes and gathers, tucks, or pleats. Ruffles and pockets are good things to look for on bodices.

The skirt portion of a dress, or a skirt, should be A-lined or gored. Stay away from straight side seams and fitted skirts, as they will buckle across the back, above the hips, and usually cup in below the hips to accent the hip area.

Empire and princess dresses are some of the most attractive silhouettes for your figure. Any style with a raised waistline or a high-fit feature will follow your body lines and be quite flattering. Choose a shirtdress with an A-line or gored skirt and long sleeves. Stay away from very blousy waistline treatments, as you should strive for smooth lines near and over the hips. A softly gathered skirt of sheer, lightweight fabric over an A-line underskirt and an underlined bodice with sheer sleeves will make a lovely dress-up look.

For a suit, select a long jacket or one that ends at the top of the hips, with an A-line or gored skirt that continues the vertical line down over the hips. Choose blouses with neck interest to wear with suits.

Large-Bust Figures

This figure type is one of the most difficult to keep in balance, proportion, and scale (figure 3–11). Sheaths and skimmers without waist seams are not for you. The front of this type of dress never hangs correctly, because so much fabric is needed to fit the bust area properly. In order to fit out the excess fabric in the skirt front area, you need a seam, so the garment can drape satisfactorily.

Choose styles with neck area interest that frame your face and carry the eye away from the bust. Drawstring necklines, softly tied bows, collars and bands, with or without buttoned front openings, will be very flattering. Any blouse or dress style that has a waist seam—high, low, or natural; a two-piece dress that can be belted to fit your natural waist or high hip; or a blouson style with a straight, fitted or softly gathered skirt should be flattering. A shirtdress with a blousy bodice and a gored skirt will be great for your figure. A belted or drawstring jacket can be your best choice for a suit.

When wearing sweaters and other knit tops, choose loosely-fitted styles with flattering U-shape or other neckline treatments to help balance your top-heavy figure.

Figure 3–10: Use styles with features at the top of the outfit to balance a Full, Round Hip Figure.

Figure 3–11: Select a smooth bodice with neckline details and a blousy waist treatment to complement a Large-Bust Figure.

Square Figures

Most slightly- or loosely-fitted styles without a waist seam will be suitable (figure 3–12). You can vary your look with a waistline treatment, but experiment first. Many square-figured women have a short back length, from neck to waist, that will need to be visually lengthened. Tie a belt at the top of the hips, or move it up and down, to find the most complementary spot. Belting a garment at the natural waistline may make a square figure look like two cubes. When making a garment with an elasticized or drawstring waist, move it up or down as seems appropriate.

Add a chic fashion touch at the neckline and upper areas of the dress or top for balance with yokes, bands, and panels with vertical lengthening lines. Add buttoned or zippered closures for versatility. Any of the necklines recommended in the Basic Dress Styles section in chapter 2 provide more options for the square-figured woman.

Straight, A-line, or gored skirts for dresses and separates will look good on a square body. Suits with jackets or vests will work well when the jacket is long, ending at the pelvic area. Separates should be selected with great care—avoid short tops and horizontal lines in the middle of the body.

Round Figure

Just about any slightly- or loosely-fitted style that does not have a waist seam will be becoming (figure 3–13). To help maintain balance and proportion, stay away from

Figure 3–12: A one-piece dress with neck and shoulder interest are figure-flattering choices for the Square Figure.

waistline seams and belts, as they will accent your widest area. If you do use a belt, tie it so that it will look like a high waistline—anywhere from two inches above the waist to just under the bust. Experiment until you find a complementary spot. When sewing, move elasticized and drawstring waistlines up. To lead the eye away from your narrow shoulders, wear set-in or raglan sleeves in any style that has a sleek look, with a minimum of fullness. Sleeveless dresses should have a bateau neckline or a high, wide, scoop. Sundress straps should fall on the outer edge of the shoulder, near the shoulder hinge.

Use fashion details at the neckline and upper portion of the bodice to balance your round figure. At the shoulders, use bands, tucks, pleats, and short yokes with gathers. Pockets and ruffles add top interest, too. For neck treatments, use any of the styles featured in Necklines in chapter 2. Front treatments such as a band, panel, curved, or diagonal seams, and button or zipper front closures add a lengthening touch.

High-waisted princess and empire silhouettes, with A-line or gored skirts, and shirtdresses that hang freely or are tied high are flattering choices. Stay away from separate skirts and two-piece dresses unless they are worn with pelvic-length tops. For suits, pick the long pelvic-length jacket over an A-line or gored skirt. For vests, try an above-the-knee length (sometimes called seven-eighths length), or one the same length as your dress or skirt.

Pants can pose special problems for round figures. Fleshy inner legs tend to rub together, pulling and distorting the pants legs while walking. Sometimes the pants legs do not fall back into place, even when you are standing still. Make sure there is adequate fabric in the thigh area of your pattern to avoid this pulling, and keep the cut of your pants legs straight.

Figure 3–13: Pick a one-piece dress that has soft, fluid lines that complement your Round Figure.

4

Color Your Wardrobe Carefully

Color is usually the first thing you notice about clothes. We all have our favorite colors to wear and to decorate our homes with. Color calls attention to itself. You are more likely to say "the woman over there in the green blouse" than "the woman over there in the placket-front French-cuffed shirt" when you are pointing someone out in a crowd. The right colors can give you a lift when you are down, help you relax when you are tense, and even make you feel a little better when you are ill. Color can profoundly affect your appearance. If you use it to change your moods and feelings in the way you decorate your home, you can certainly use it to change your appearance.

As you plan your new, flattering wardrobe, you will need a working knowledge of color. Fabrics and accessories, plus hair color and cosmetics, need to be chosen to complement your figure, skin, and eye color. Never choose a color just because you think it is pretty, or because your best friend looks great in it. The use of color can be so subtle that one shade of blue may enhance your complexion and figure, while the same color only a shade lighter will make you look bulky and washed-out. The right color for you, obviously, will make your garment more attractive. Meticulous sewing and a good fit often go unnoticed because the color of the fabric is all wrong for the wearer. Color is *that* important.

Spring and fall, fashion designers, fashion magazines, fabric companies, and cosmetic companies all promote new colors for the season, to create some additional excitement along with the new styles. It is a lot of fun, and while we all cannot afford to assemble a new wardrobe each season, adding at least one new item in a new style or color can make you feel better. But here is where you must first be true to yourself. Your special size must, of course, be considered when assessing new styles and deciding if they can be made to work for you. The season's new colors may all be impossible for you, attractive as they are. If this is the case, *always* stick to your own best colors. Make that new style in *your* best color, not fashion's latest. You will look much better and have a garment that will be wearable with other color-planned items in your closet.

Start thinking about how you can make color work for you as you read this chapter. You will learn about the twelve basic colors—primary, secondary, and tertiary, and all the values in between. You will discover you can create optical illusions with color, and you will learn how to choose your best colors. Knowing what styles are best for you and how to pick the right fabrics (chapter 5) are technical aspects of dressing well. Color is the exciting, dramatic part, the touch that literally can make or break your look.

Understanding Color

There are twelve basic colors. Thousands upon thousands of other colors can be made by blending these basics together in different quantities and combinations. The twelve basics begin with three pure, or primary, colors. These are blended to form three more colors, called secondary colors; finally, the primary and secondary colors are blended in equal amounts to create

six tertiary colors. From these twelve, the whole color spectrum evolves.

Most of the colors used to dye fabrics are blended in huge amounts. When even a tiny bit more of one color in a recipe is added, this vat of dye can color fabric that is noticeably different from fabric dyed in another vat, using the same recipe. If you knit, you know this already, and always buy all your yarn at the same time and from the same dye lot. This slight difference in dye blends also holds true for fabrics. Colors can and do vary from manufacturer to manufacturer. You may have several navy blue garments in your present wardrobe that do not match or look good together. The reason this happens is because the navy garments were made with different dye lots, all called navy blue. One navy may seem to have a reddish or greenish cast, while another may be purplish in tone, depending upon the amounts of the basic colors used in blending this shade. Realizing that there are such differences within the same color makes you more aware of the differences between colors. Beauty may be in the eye of the beholder, but it is the color of the clothes that we all see first.

Primary Colors

Red, Blue and Yellow are the three foundation colors, the bases for all other colors. These three basics are bright colors, and for most large women, or those with figures lacking ideal proportions,

only touches of these colors should be used. Their brightness tends to make them draw specific attention. For example, a bright red skirt will emphasize large hips. Accessories and jewelry in brilliant primary colors are smart ways to perk up an outfit.

Secondary Colors

Orange, Green and Purple are created from equal amounts of two primary colors: for orange, red and yellow are blended; for green, blue and yellow; for purple, red and blue.

Most larger women should stay away from these rich, secondary colors, because they are attention-getters. However, if you have an outgoing personality and are large, but in proportion, there is no reason why you cannot use any of the six primary and secondary colors for a dramatic fashion statement, as long as the garment's lines are flattering. For an understated look, choose darker shades or lighter shades of these colors.

Tertiary Colors

When equal amounts of the primary and secondary colors are mixed, six more colors are created: Yellow-Orange, Red-Orange, Red-Violet, Yellow-Green, Blue-Green, and Blue-Violet. Since these colors are somewhat softer than the primary and secondary colors, they are good choices if you like strong color, but figure flaws prevent you from wearing too much bold color.

If these colors—primary, secondary, tertiary—are confusing, one way to make sense of them and acquire some first-hand color knowledge for yourself is to get some paints—acrylic, oil, even water colors—at an art supply store and experiment. Buy only the primary colors—red, yellow and blue—and black and white. Start mixing the primaries in equal amounts to create secondary and tertiary colors. Then, add black and white to these mixtures to create light and dark shades. You'll soon understand the components of color, as well as how to evaluate color.

Evaluating Color

Having a map is great, but unless you know how to use it, a map is just another interesting picture. The same holds true for color. The days are long gone when colored fabrics were limited in range. Modern technology gives us dyes and fabrics in every imaginable hue. If you are going to make the most of the colors that are available, it is important that you know how to analyze them. Evaluating color by *value* (lightness or darkness), *shade*, or by *intensity* (brightness or dullness) gives you the basic how-to's for putting colors together.

Value

The value of a color is its lightness or darkness, often called *shade*. The lighter values are colors to which white has been added—fashion designers call these colors pastels. The darker colors are those to which black has been added. Think of the color red. A light-value red, with white added, is pink. A dark-value red, with black added, is maroon. Now imagine these three colors side by side—pink, red and maroon—and you can easily see what color value means.

Shade

Shades of colors, especially in the darker range, are usually figure-flattering choices for larger women. Lighter shades, because of the white added, tend to reflect light and can make your figure look larger. The darker shades, because of the added black, tend to absorb light, making your figure look somewhat smaller.

Intensity

In addition to being light or dark, a color can be bright or dull. Go back to thinking of pink. Now think of the color hot pink. While both colors have a light value, the hot pink is much brighter, or more intense, than plain pink. For an example of a dull pink, think, if you can, of the pink of a rhododendron flower. It is a muted, soft pink, much duller than hot pink or plain pink.

Why is all this information about value and intensity important? Because it enables you to put colors together well. While the combining of colors is sometimes just a matter of taste (some women like purple and red together; others cannot stand that combination), the rules cannot be rigid. But to be sure you are in good taste, value and intensity considerations do provide important guidelines: mix values (shades) but not intensities. Translation: Do not mix a bright color with a dull one. Pale blue (light and dull) and navy (dark and dull) is a great combination; hot pink (light and intense) and maroon (dark and dull) is not. Colors of the same intensity work well together, such as the pale blue and navy, or hot pink and fuchsia. You may wish to think in terms of shiny and dull surfaces. They do not really look good together, either.

Another important aspect of color intensity is the way light is absorbed or reflected. Larger figures look better in colors that absorb light. Dull colors, especially darker ones, absorb light, while brighter ones reflect light, just like a shiny surface. The same person, for example, in a hot-pink dress will look a few sizes larger than she would if she were wearing the same dress in a soft, dusty pink, a dull color—still very pretty—but one that tends to absorb more light.

How to Find Your Best Colors

Color can be your best friend or worst enemy. The right color can make you look radiant and healthy, while another color can make you look ill or tired. Is one of your favorite outfits a comfortable dark red pantsuit or a brown shirtdress? Think about your favorite outfit and why you like it. Its design flatters you; the fabric is comfortable and you like the way it makes you look. Does its color make you look glowing and pretty? Examine the color of this outfit closely. Is it reddish, bluish, or yellowish in tone? If it is red, or has an inclination toward red, pull out some other garments you own that are in the red range and hold them near your face. These colors probably also flatter your skin, eyes, and hair. If your favorite outfit is blue, you probably look good in colors with a lot of blue in them. If you have trouble determining your best colors this way, you might want to start testing basic colors—red, blue, yellow—as they are, then proceed from there.

Testing Colors

If you cannot find a color category among the clothes in your wardrobe now, use other items—scarves, table linens—anything you have around in the colors you want to test. It will be a startling revelation as you notice how some colors appear to do nothing for you, while others seem to make your complexion and eyes brighter. For example, you may have a comfortable pink blouse that you love to wear, but every time you do, someone asks you if you are feeling ill. Most likely there is too much purple or yellow in the shade of pink, which emphasizes the sallow, yellow tones of your skin. On the other hand, you may have a blouse in a different shade of pink that seems to call forth compliments, because it does wonders for your figure and gives your skin a healthy glow. There are also colors which would not logically seem to work with the color of your skin, but the color of your eyes comes alive when you wear that color. Since there are no rules that can safely be followed as far as skin color and clothing color, you just

have to experiment. Be sure to test colors with natural or incandescent lighting. Fluorescent light distorts red tones and cannot give you a true color reading.

Stand in front of a well-lighted full-length mirror and drape the fabric sample around your neck to see how it affects your skin and hair. If the fabric sample is large enough, drape it over your shoulders (or put it on if it is one of your garments) and around your body (figure 4-1). As you try each color, ask yourself these questions:

1. Does it do anything for my overall appearance?

2. Does it make my eyes brighter? Duller?

3. Does it make my skin look clear? Harsh? Washed-out? Glow?

4. Does it make my hair seem lustrous? Dull?

5. Does it reflect a true image of my body? Does it make me look somewhat smaller? Or does the color seem to make me look larger?

Select only those colors that seem the most flattering. If you are not sure, get a friend's opinion. You may find that your best colors all have the same hue to them, either red, blue, or yellow. In the beginning it may be wise to pick one color and use it to build a foundation for a working color scheme. You will undoubtedly find many prints, plaids, stripes, and other variations that will go with your foundation color, when you begin to put color together. You will soon be amazed at your expertise as you eliminate colors because there is too much red, yellow, or blue in your test samples.

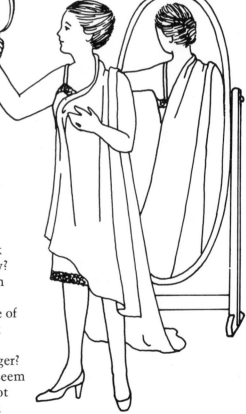

Figure 4-1

Putting Colors Together

How many times have you seen someone wearing a really nice out-fit, made up of two or more colors that blended together perfectly—and you wondered what her secret was in being able to put clothes together so well. Think again the next time you see such an outfit, and you will immediately under-stand its skillful use of color.

One-Color Dressing

I know of a woman who wears only shades of purple. All her ac-cessories are purple, too, and how she manages that without getting bored is a mystery. Her fashion statement seems a little limited, but she certainly does not have to worry about combining different colors.

One-color dressing is a good way to create a foundation for your wardrobe. Choose the color that looks best on you and put together an outfit or two in that color—skirt, or slacks and blouse, or sweater and dress. Then build on that basic color with other items and accessories in lighter or darker shades of your basic color, or with prints, plaids, or stripes that have a lot of your basic color in them. Also, keep the shades of your basic color in the same tones. For example, if your basic color is a warm reddish-brown, be sure all your coordinating wardrobe items have the same warm tones. This means that a yellowish-beige blouse will not work as well with a reddish-brown skirt as will a pinkish-beige blouse. Mixing inten-sities is something to be avoided: keep soft shades of the same color together and keep bright shades of the same color together. Unless you are convinced that you only look good in one color, like the purple-clad woman, use one-color dressing only as a foundation on which to build your wardrobe.

Contrasting With Caution

Two contrasting colors are those that are not created from the same basic color. In other words, red and green are contrasting colors because red is a primary color, and green a secondary color made from blue and yellow. Yellow (primary) and purple (made from red and blue) are also contrasting, as are blue (primary) and orange (made from red and yel-low). Conversely, orange (red and yellow) and purple (red and blue) are not contrasting colors, because they share the color red.

Since contrasting colors are usu-ally strong colors, you might want to exercise caution in wearing such combinations, even in their lighter shades. The contrast could create horizontal lines and direct attention to problem figure areas. But if you enjoy strong color, use contrasting colors for a suit blouse, hat, or ac-cent, such as a scarf or jewelry. For the bold, try a contrasting front panel in a princess-seamed dress that has no waistline. The vertical lines are slenderizing, and the fashion statement is a knockout.

If you want to put lighter shades of contrasting colors together, be-ware of the different tones of color you might find in lighter and/or darker shades of your basic color. These tones, which come from the recipe used in dying the fabric, or other finishes, might be strong enough to throw off your contrast. Even with white fabrics you might find some problems. Often white fabric is treated with a bluing agent to make it look pure white and not yellowish on the bolt, but when you make a blouse out of such a white fabric and put it next to your fa-vorite navy skirt, that bluish tone is noticeable and you have no true contrast in colors.

Harmonizing Colors

These are colors which, although different, contain at least one similar primary color. Yellow (primary) and orange (made from red and yellow) are harmonizing colors, as are green (blue and yellow) and blue (primary). Har-monizing colors are more difficult to put together, because the dye mix of a fabric can make a color that should perfectly harmonize with another, clash. Colors harmonize well that have the same tone to them—bluish green and bluish gray, for example. Harmonizing colors are best for large sizes because they do not call attention to themselves as do contrasting colors.

Neutrals

So far the discussion has focused on major colors and how to use them in terms of fashion. But fash-ion has recognized, indeed holds in high regard, a category of color called neutrals: black, white, gray, brown, and beige. Various mixtures of the primary and secondary colors are used to create these colors. Neutrals are safe, always fashionable and tasteful, and especially appropriate for large sizes. They are not as difficult to put together as other colors (although watch the color tones some neutrals have), and are not at all attention-getting. You could even say they recede into the background. But as easy as these colors are to work with, they can be difficult to wear well. While a soft-pink blouse may make you look healthy, a classic beige one, since yellow is the basic color in beige, may make you look jaundiced. White, black, and gray, because of their starkness, may be the worst thing for sallow or very pale complexions. Even if black makes you look three sizes smaller, it can also make you look near death if it is not compatible with your skin tones.

Combine neutrals with other colors, or look for neutrals with color casts that favor you. Gray, for example, can have a bluish or pinkish cast, either one flattering to a skin complemented by red or blue. Even brown can have a yellowish or reddish cast, so choose your neutrals carefully. Neutrals can be used for one-color dressing, with accents of other colors (see next section).

Since neutrals go well with other colors, this color group is a good choice for main wardrobe items—winter coats, raincoats, shoes, boots, handbags, and belts. Unless you do not feel confident wearing major colors, do not make a neutral your basic wardrobe color. Use neutrals to expand your wardrobe, because that is what they do best.

Using Color as an Accent

The best way to make any outfit more interesting is to add an accent of some sort, some item of a different color that will catch the eye. While combining colors uses logic, adding accent colors requires imagination. Accent colors can be used to take emphasis away from one area of the body and place it somewhere else. A colorful scarf can draw attention away from large hips. Piping or trim on a skirt can divert attention from a large bust. Accent colors can be in the form of jewelry, a scarf, belt, hat, gloves, handbag, or some part of a garment, such as piping, buttons, binding, facings, appliqués, embroidery, even collars and cuffs of a different color.

Try to keep all your accent colors within tasteful limits, as too much of a good thing is worse than nothing at all. Trims can be used as accents, too, such as lace edging or ribbon trim used to define a collar, placket, or cuffs. Place your trims carefully, without putting too much emphasis on horizontal lines, which can make you look larger. Keep accent trims fairly narrow. For example, rows of ⅛-inch ribbon running down a summer skirt are far more slenderizing than two or three rows of 1-inch ribbon similarly placed. If you like accents but worry about too much contrast in color, select harmonizing colors or matching colors. The difference in texture between the trim and the garment fabric will catch the eye.

Color for an Optical Illusion

While your measurements are a fact, you can help the eye to see not so much a large woman but a well-dressed one. When you experimented with color to find your most flattering shades, you no doubt noticed that some of the colors created an illusion of a longer, sleeker body. Color can help you de-emphasize a figure flaw or imperfect body proportions—even colors other than black, brown, and navy. Some of the lighter, more subdued shades in the cool color group—blue, green, purple, gray, yellow-green, blue-green and blue-violet have a tendency to minimize, as can dull colors in almost every shade. Fabric design, too, can create an optical illusion of vertical, slenderizing lines. Small prints, uneven plaids with dominant vertical bars and small vertical stripes will also help create a taller, smoother image. Prints with harmonizing or muted colors may give a one-color illusion. Harmonizing vertical stripes in your best colors will have a narrowing effect, but stay away from broad, bright stripes that could give an illusion of greater girth. Textured fabric, in a flattering color, with vertical ribs, will also help to create a more slender illusion.

For the greatest illusion of height, color should seem to flow from the shoulders to the hem in smooth, vertical lines. This is easily done with one-color dressing—a blue suit, for example, with a blouse in a lighter shade of blue, or a brown jumper with a lighter beige blouse. You are not limited, though, to one-color dressing. You can use contrasting or harmonizing fabrics, along with a solid color, in prints, stripes, or plaids with a vertical design. Always start with your best colors and build from there.

You can learn a lot by looking at other people; so when you see color combinations that are pleasing, make a mental note to find out if those colors will work for you as well.

Creating Illusions With Color by Figure Type

Contrasting trim around a neckline and/or down the front of a dress or blouse will add vertical interest for *all five figure types*. Jumpers, one-color garments, are a very flattering style for all five figure types, especially if worn with one of the open necklines suggested in chapter 2. Wear a contrasting color blouse, in a lightweight fabric, with long, fitted, or shirt-type sleeves. Another vertical color illusion for all five figure types is long, colored scarves or long necklaces, neither of which should be worn knotted close to the neck.

Dresses with contrasting collars add interest to the top of the body, creating an illusion of balance for the full, round hip figure. Wear light-color tops and blouses with dark skirts and slacks, or use one-color dressing, adding collar accents to the top half of your body. Large-bust figures can usually wear skirts or pants with contrasting piping, or other trims, on pockets. This figure type can wear tops that are no more than a shade or two lighter than skirts and pants. Avoid dark tops and blouses with light-color skirts and pants, as this only works well with perfectly proportioned figures. One-color dressing can minimize a top-heavy figure quite well. Women with square, round, and rectangular figures should stay away from bright, light separates worn with intense, dark separates. The contrasting overblouse and pants outfit worn by so many large women only adds to their girth. The best vertical illusion for these three figure types is created with jackets, vests, and sweaters in the same colors or in colors just slightly different from the skirts or pants. Vary the look with muted tweeds, checks, plaids, stripes, prints, or textured fabrics—as long as the fabric projects a continuing vertical line. Use contrasting colors for accents or accessories, or for such items as a blouse under a suit or jumper. Never cut the body in half with drastic color changes at the waist on any of these three figure types, as the break creates a horizontal line that is in no way flattering.

Color to Create a Mood

Certain colors are considered cool, serene, and low-key, and others warm, stimulating, and outgoing. This is basically controlled by the dominant primary color. As you become aware of the many facets of color, you will perceive which shade or color looks cool and which warm. All of the colors considered cool contain some level of blue, and practically no red at all. Warm colors contain some red and almost no blue; the third primary color, yellow, can be in either warm or cool shades.

Colors create a mood. If you are an extrovert, you will probably enjoy warm colors in your home and wardrobe. If you are shy, you probably feel most comfortable wearing cool, reserved colors, and surrounded by neutral colors in your home.

Cool Colors: Blue, green, and purple, yellow-green, blue-green, and blue-violet—all colors containing some blue and practically no red—are thought of as cool colors. The bright, intense shades—emerald, turquoise, lime—work well as colors for accessories and accents, while the darker, more muted shades—navy, hunter green—can be basic colors in your wardrobe. When you want to present a cool, understated appearance, wear an icy blue or green outfit. For a cool, regal look, make a garment in your most complementary shade of purple. For the office, cool colors are a good choice. The darker cool colors are usually flattering to large figures, and these colors are generally considered more "serious" than warm colors. A good, businesslike image is conveyed with garments of navy, dark green, and the many other shades of blue.

Warm Colors: Red, orange, and yellow—as well as yellow-orange, red-orange, and red-violet—all with little or no blue, are the foundations of the warm color group. These lively, bright colors can be good warming balances for some of the cool colors in your wardrobe, when used for hats, blouses, scarves, and other accessories. For a cold winter night, put on a bright red or orange caftan for relaxing by the fire, or to light up a party. The warming power of the red or orange will soon make you feel as bright and cheerful as you look. If you live in a southern climate, wear a reddish-yellow garment on damp, rainy nights or for a stimulating evening out. These radiant colors are attention-getters. Be cautious about using them indiscriminately in your special size.

Hair Color and Style

Clean, silky hair in a becoming color and style is as important as any piece of clothing. Even an old outfit looks good if your hair is well-groomed and flattering. Fashions can either be enhanced or, sometimes, overwhelmed by your hairstyle. If you decide to change your hair color, the new shade should add highlights and sheen to your hair without clashing with your skin and eyes. Look at your skin. Its color will guide you in selecting a hair color. If your skin is sallow, olive, or gray-looking, stay away from blonde, as it will emphasize the yellow aspects of your skin and make you look ill. Use a highlighting technique instead, or add reddish or brunette tones for the warm-

ing effect your skin needs. If you have a pink or pale complexion, you will probably be a lovely blonde. If you have gray hair and want to keep it, examine your face to see if the gray complements or makes you look washed-out. If it is not flattering in its present state, you can put a toning rinse on it to even out the color and make it more vibrant, but avoid the bluish tones that for some reason many women add to their gray hair. Consult with a professional colorist if you are not sure about any change in hair color.

Hair styles, like everything else used to create a balanced fashion in pleasing proportions, should be neither too long nor too short on a large woman. Depending on the shape of your face, you will want to frame it with a style that complements the shape of your face and adds fullness where necessary. A style that is too flat will make the body look that much bigger in relation to the head. If the hair is too full, the head will look small under all that hair and the body will look even bigger. Despite its vertical lines, straight, long hair, that hangs below the shoulders and lies on the bosom often makes the head look smaller, and if the hair fans out, it creates an unpleasing widening effect where it ends. Instead, try a shoulder or chin length that can be brushed upward or held in place at the sides for an upswept line that will add to a vertical look. The fashion of wearing sun glasses on top of your head, with the hair tucked behind your ears, is a flattering, lengthening style that goes well with casual

clothes and sportswear. You can achieve the same effect with headbands and scarves tied around the head in this manner. Long hair wrapped close to the head can also make your head look smaller and your body larger. Hair heavily teased into an exaggerated bouffant style or piled high like a beehive is not at all flattering to a large woman, as these styles only emphasize bulk.

Chin-length or slightly longer hairstyles in a bowl cut, feather-cut, or curly permanent that can be blown dry have many variations that will flatter every facial shape. An attractive variation for almost every length is to use barrettes or combs to pull the hair up away from the ears, toward the back, in a soft upsweep to create an upward line.

Short, flat hair can be the downfall of the large woman. Haircuts that outline the shape of the head only succeed in making the head appear smaller on a large body. An all-over two- to three-inch length that has been curled or is naturally wavy is adequate to frame the face and not project the look of a disproportionately small head. Women with long hair who like to wear it up in a French twist or chignon should create a frame around the face with wisps of hair, curls, or braids, or puff up the hair enough to soften the look.

Cosmetics

We are constantly being bombarded with carefully created magazine advertisements and subtly choreographed TV commercials about the wonders of many cosmetic products. While these products cannot perform miracles, what they can do is make you feel better about the way you look. Since many of the cosmetic companies, especially the better ones, offer free makeup demonstrations, why not take advantage of some of these promotions. Go to the store, get a makeup demonstration, ask questions. After all, they want you to buy and be happy with their products. But if you cannot bring yourself to do this alone in a store, do some research on your own. You can find books available on makeup application, and articles in many of the women's magazines include instructions on skillful makeup application. When you start to experiment on your own, try different shades for each area: skin, cheeks, eyes, and lips. Enlist a friend. You can apply makeup to each other, as well as pool your current makeup collections so you will not have to purchase colors your friend may have.

The natural look—like you are not wearing makeup at all—is still the most desirable one for the large woman. Learn to accent your best features well and with subtlety, which is the essence of the natural look. Cosmetics may affect your clothing color selections for some occasions, so choose and use them wisely. (For example, do not wear purple eye shadow with a peach evening gown.) Nature can always use a little help. Apply cosmetic

colors with a light touch so you do not look painted or artificial. While you can get a healthy glow from subtly used foundations and blushers, no matter where you live—warm or cold climate—some moisturizing is needed. Skin care is even more important than color cosmetics. Indeed, if you only used a good moisturizer regularly, you might not even want or need to use color cosmetics. Moisturizers keep the skin supple, protect it from weather, and generally make you look younger. Next to cleansing, it is the most important aspect of skin care.

When choosing cosmetic colors, choose the foundation makeup nearest to your own color (going a shade darker, rather than lighter) that will give you an added glow. Apply foundation sparingly and be sure to blend it down under the chin, as far down as your dress or blouse neckline. There is nothing more disconcerting than to see an abrupt line where makeup stops. Blushers and rouge need to be carefully applied, too. Place a dot at the intersection of the line created downward from the middle of your eye and outward from the tip of your nose, blending the color upward into the temples. For some women, besides carefully blended cheek color, a touch of color on the forehead and chin helps. Try this little trick of mine: after you have blended the rouge or blusher on the cheeks, remove the excess from your fingertips by gently stroking them over your chin and forehead for a healthy flush.

Your eyes can be your best feature, so take special care. Find an eye shadow that seems to brighten your eyes, not necessarily one that matches your eyes or your outfit. Gentle, contrasting colors are usually pretty, or colors that pick up one of the flecks of color in your eyes. Remember that the subtle touch is best. You want people to look at your eyes, not your eye makeup. Use flesh-colored, cover-up cream to camouflage puffiness or dark circles under your eyes. When using eye liner, stay away from extremely dark or harsh colors. Apply a moderately-toned liner that matches your eyelashes and harmonizes with your eye shadow.

Lipstick colors should blend with the rest of your makeup. Use pinkish or reddish shades with pinkish rouges and blushers, peach or brownish shades with those tones of makeup. Color on the lips is the only makeup some women use, and this practice only succeeds in making the rest of the face look washed-out. Be aware that even your most flattering garment may clash with your lipstick if the lipstick color is not carefully chosen.

If you have changed the color of your hair, you may also have to change your makeup to suit your new look. With brighter hair colors—reds, brunettes, golden browns—you can use brighter, deeper cosmetic colors. If your hair is gray or pale, use soft, receding colors; otherwise, you may look garish.

5

Fabric for the Ample Figure

An impressive fashion statement always begins with a meticulously selected fabric. The right color and texture will enhance the wearer's appearance. The fabric must be the one best for the pattern's style lines. In chapter 1, you learned how to realistically evaluate your figure. Chapter 2 helped you select design silhouettes with the kind of fashion details that look well-balanced and in proportion, while at the same time using those design lines to create a more attractive fashion image. The not-so-deep mysteries of pattern selection were revealed in chapter 3, enabling you to choose figure-flattering styles. Your personal color scheme for your wardrobe was explored in chapter 4, listing all the information needed to help you pick your most becoming colors. And now, you are ready to learn how to select the right fabrics.

How do you make the right fabric decisions? Think like a designer. When purchasing fabric, consider every aspect—fabric thickness, texture, color, even the size of a print or stripe. Here are the four most important guidelines to keep in mind when buying fabric:

1. Suitability for pattern design: Will the fabric be too soft or too crisp? Is this a pattern for knits only? Is a plaid or stripe appropriate?

2. Flattering color and surface treatment: Should blouse and skirt colors be the same? Would a velveteen be too bulky for a large size? Would a dull-surface fabric look better on a large bust than a shiny fabric?

3. Comfort and care requirements: Is ironing or dry cleaning out of the question? Natural fibers are most comfortable, but are you willing to give them the special care they sometimes require?

4. Quality as reflected in workmanship, color, and durability: Is the fabric evenly dyed? Are there visible runs, slubs, or pulls?

Purchasing Tips

When you walk into a fabric shop or department, it is easy to be overwhelmed by the great variety of fascinating yard goods on display. Take some time to examine the different types available. Touch and run your hands over the fabrics as they drape invitingly from the bolts and rolls. Take time to explore all the possible choices. This is the only way to find the best fabric for you and your pattern.

To make the right choice for your next sewing project, let us review the pertinent points: suitability for pattern design lines; the figure flattering aspects of the material's color and surface texture; comfort and care requirements; and quality. *Do Not* make a purchase until you have reviewed these four guidelines. After a while, applying these guidelines will become almost automatic as you shop for fabric. Be aware of all of the options as you consider each purchase and stay away from compromise. Find another fabric if your first choice is not suitable for your pattern, or find another pattern that will look splendid made in that particular fabric. Even the most skilled seamstress cannot make a garment look good on her figure if the fabric has not been carefully and appropriately chosen.

Suitability

Ask yourself the following questions:

1. Is the fabric suitable for the pattern's style lines? The pattern's designer created a definite silhouette, as you can see by the sketch or photograph on the pattern envelope. Whether fitted or loose, or somewhere in between, the style will look its best made in certain types of fabrics. The fabric suggestions on the envelope tell you that either a soft or crisp fabric is recommended, and lists examples. Occasionally, both soft and crisp fabrics will be suitable.

A fabric that is limp or droopy (soft) will not hold the shape of a design recommended for crisp fabrics—for example, a sculptured A-line or fitted dress. Conversely, garments recommended for soft, drapable fabrics just will not work in a fabric that is stiff and cannot be gathered into soft, fluid lines.

Both woven and knit fabrics can have either soft or crisp characteristics. Sometimes you will have to take an especially close look to tell the knits and wovens apart. Knit manufacturers have invented new ways of making knits; so the fabrics retain the comfort of knits but have the appearance of woven fabrics.

To determine if a fabric is *Soft* or *Crisp*, hold about a yard of the fabric in one hand, letting it hang down free and undisturbed. Soft fabrics will fall in small folds in a straight line; crisp fabrics will make round, rolling folds, fanning outward near the free edge (figure 5–1).

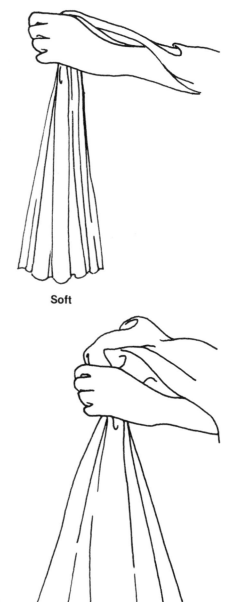

Soft

Crisp

Figure 5–1: Select fabric that has draping qualities that will help to retain the design's silhouette.

2. Will the fabric complement your figure? You can test the fabric in the store before you buy it. To see if a particular fabric suits you, take the fabric bolt to a full-length, well-lighted mirror. Hold the fabric under your chin to see how the color works with your complexion and hair. Next, drape several yards of the fabric down, over, and around your body. Do not be shy about doing this. After all, it is your money you will be spending. Check to see if the color and draping qualities (see question 1) are right for you and your figure.

Does the fabric complement your figure with its particular thickness, texture, or design? Could a printed motif possibly fall at an inappropriate spot? A splash of flowers on a large print may work to emphasize large hips or bust. Does the design run crosswise, seeming to pull your glance from right to left, giving the illusion of added width?

Further along in this chapter you will learn more specific details about knits and wovens, fabric thickness, stripes, plaids and checks, prints, solids, and special fabrics such as napped surfaces, sheers and lace, satin and crepe—all of which will be of great help when selecting fabric. But first, some information on soft and crisp fabrics and what they can do for, or to, your figure.

Soft Knitted Fabrics

The ample-figured woman should choose soft knits with extreme care, as these fabrics tend to cling to the body and reveal unsightly curves and bulges. Garments that are slightly- or loosely-fitted designs, with style ease, are the best choices. You may also find garments that are a combination of fitted styles that work well in a soft knit for some types of large figures. This type of garment could be a loosely-fitted blouson dress, with a fitted skirt—best for a *large-busted* woman, for example—or a semifitted bodice with loosely-fitted skirt, a good style for a *large-hipped* woman.

Easily recognizable soft knitted fabrics are polyester or nylon interlocks, jerseys, and tricots. There are also knitted sheers and lace looks which are quite soft and clingy. On the scene, too, are luxurious silk and wool knits, perfect for dressier outfits.

Soft Woven Fabrics

The full-figured woman will find soft woven fabrics do not cling or droop as soft knits will. Soft woven fabrics have just enough body to allow the fabric to glide over the figure without emphasizing the very areas that need to be camouflaged. Styles for soft wovens should be semifitted, slightly-fitted, or loosely-fitted, as these fabrics cannot bear much strain. Fitted styles in soft wovens will tend to pull out or fray at the seams if the garment is too closely fitted, due to body pressure as you move around.

Soft wovens include many elegant fabrics such as silk, hankerchief linen, flannel, tissue wools, crepe, beautiful designer cottons and cotton blends, plus domestic calico-look blends, voile, batiste, shantung, pongee, and many other synthetics and blends that emulate the classic, natural fabrics with their soft, drapy qualities.

Crisp Knitted Fabrics

This type of knit has become the favorite of all who like comfortable, classic—even tailored—clothes. Their wash-and-wear characteristics, along with the comfortable "give" built in to most knits appeal to big women (and men) of all ages. Any style silhouette that has a definite shape, such as gored or A-line skirts or fitted jackets, works well for crisp knits. *Do Not* overfit, however, because then you will define all the figure flaws you want to conceal. Crisp knits are not meant to be gathered or draped, as crisp wovens are not. They should be used for styles with few gathers or minimal, eased fullness.

The most popular crisp knitted fabrics are plain, crepe or pebble doubleknits, suit-weight jerseys and interlocks, and other types of crisp doubleknits that may have surfaces that look like denim, velvet, corduroy, or other woven fabrics.

Crisp Woven Fabrics

Any crisp woven fabric can be used advantageously by the large woman. But, it can cause problems with proportions if the fabric stands away from the body, making the eye move across the body, seeming to add bulk or girth. Crisp wovens are best for styles that have simple lines in a fitted or semifitted silhouette, with vertical emphasis. Stay away from heavily gathered or draped styles. Crisp wovens will hold the sharp creases of pressed pleats and are the best choice for beautifully tailored clothing. Crisp fabrics also work well with fashion details, such as prominent curved or diagonal seams, because they hold the garment shape without drooping. Ginghams and other cottons with crisp characteristics look great in unpressed, A-shape pleated skirts, as the pleats may be pressed flat over the hip area to eliminate some bulk. A crisp fabric will take a bit of gathering when made as a fitted A-line skirt (as explained in the skirt section of Pattern Variations in chapter 6).

Crisp wovens may be as thin as organdy or as thick as denim or corduroy. Other crisp wovens you will recognize are kettlecloth, taffeta, twill, satin, most suiting fabrics, butcher linen, chino, brocade, duck, gabardine, piqué, poplin, and serge.

Knits vs. Wovens

The two basic kinds of fabric are knits and wovens. Knits are produced on needles that form the yarns into chains and rows of loops. A modern knitting machine can produce fabric up to 168 inches wide, can knit 1,000 courses (cross rows), and make 4,700,000 stitches per minute, an unheard-of possibility not too long ago. These knitting machines can make fabric two to five times faster than a weaving loom can make woven fabrics, plus create many intricate and lacy patterns from the yarns.

Wovens are produced by two sets of yarns interlaced at right angles. Lengthwise, the threads are called the warp, crosswise, the weft. Modern techniques include shuttleless looms that can pick (weave over and under lengthwise threads) at a speed of up to 440 picks a minute. Garment textiles are woven up to 72 inches wide, while bed sheets and other household fabrics are woven 80 or more inches wide.

There are thousands of fabric varieties in which different textures, patterns, and surface finishes are added during the manufacturing and weaving processes, sometimes making it hard to tell if a fabric is woven or knitted. If you are not sure which it is, simply pull a thread at the cut end. As the thread runs crosswise, loops will appear in a knit; straight thread ends (almost fringelike) will be revealed in wovens.

Knits

We are all now familiar with the many types of knits, but each has two main characteristics: *ribs* are the lengthwise rows of loops; *courses* are the crosswise loops that run from selvage to selvage, or horizontally in tube knits. Ribs are the equivalent of the lengthwise grain (warp), and courses the crosswise grain (weft) we are so familiar with in wovens.

Knits have more ''give'' than most woven fabrics, making them more comfortable for larger figures to wear. But do not fall into the trap that catches so many big women. Do *not* use the knit's stretching quality in place of wearing ease. A

knit garment that is too tight reveals all your figure flaws and may give you the appearance of a stuffed sausage!

Pay particular attention to the fabric suggestions on your pattern envelope when purchasing knits. *Firm, stable knits* that do not have much stretch may be used for almost any type of garment; *stretchable knits* have patterns specifically designed for them. Garments designed for *stretchable knits only* have less wearing ease than other styles, which may make you want to think twice about such a garment. This means these styles have a closer fit, which could be too tight and revealing for a large woman.

Wovens

This type of fabric has lengthwise threads (warp) that are interlaced with crosswise threads (weft), creating many different surface patterns and textures. Since wovens have straight threads, rather than looped yarns like knits, they are more rigid than knits. This factor must be considered when purchasing. This may also make knits a better choice for the large woman.

Wovens offer a greater variety of types of fabrics than knits, however, due to the three weaving methods used to create different wovens: plain (straight crosswise and lengthwise threads), twill (a diagonal weave), and satin (a weave with extra long ''floats'' of threads on the face side, usually on the warp). These weaves allow the use of yarns that may have thick-and-thin slub effects, crimping, twisting, looping, and curling. Familiar wovens range from sheer, thin, and transparent fabrics to very thick and rich fabrics. Organdy, voile, crepe, broadcloth, shantung, gabardine, bouclé, velveteen, corduroy, denim, and tweed are just a few examples of the wide variety of different types of wovens.

The modern wovens we have become so familiar with, such as permanent-press fabrics of cotton or rayon and polyester, are blends with easy-care properties that emulate classic natural-fiber fabrics. But the classic woven naturals—cotton, linen, silk, and wool—are being rediscovered by fashion in a big way. Your challenge will be to select the one which will be right for you.

Figure Flattery: Surface and Color Treatments

Because of the many surface and design variations, each characteristic influences the total fashion look. You need to know more about these fabric features to make satisfactory choices.

Fabric Thickness

Since there are so many ways fabric surface can be created, you should think first about the fabric's thickness. For example, gingham is a thin fabric that everyone recognizes; denim is medium-thick, and corduroy ranges from medium-thick to very thick. Knits may be any thickness from very thin or sheer to quite thick. Other fabrics may be

rather thin but have raised, thick designs woven in (brocades, cut velvets, flocked fabrics), in which case these materials are considered thick fabrics. Your main concern with fabric thickness is what it will do for your figure.

In choosing thin fabrics you need to think mainly about color, design, quality, durability, and comfort. Most thin fabrics, especially wovens, will be flattering to you. Medium-thick fabrics will also flatter, unless they have unusual surface treatments, such as strong horizontal patterns which could make you look bulky. Certain thick fabrics are bound to add weight to your already ample figure; so select them with care or avoid them altogether, except for winter coats.

Now that you are aware of fabric thickness and its ability to affect your appearance, consider the surface treatments of various fabrics in solid colors and what surface and color can do for you.

Texture and Color

A solid-color fabric can be the large woman's best friend, especially when receding colors are worn. But colors must be carefully combined with fabric textures. A fuzzy, furlike finish on a coat, even in your best color, may make you look pounds heavier, while a vertical rib (woven or knitted) fabric coat will be slenderizing. Solid-color fabrics are the foundation of a flattering wardrobe, providing you many options for shades of color and different textures. But not all solid colors are for you, nor are all

textures. Review the preceding section on fabric thickness as you think about your figure and fabrics.

The rectangular-shaped figure will be able to wear most thin to medium-thick fabrics. Just stay away from horizontally ribbed fabrics, such as ottoman, and similar fabrics that may add girth. Why not experiment with several solid-color fabrics with different surface treatments while in front of the store mirror? You may be overlooking a fabric that will look splendid on you.

The figure with a narrow top and full, round hips should stay with thin to medium-thick fabrics. An outfit with a slightly-fitted velour top and a denim skirt, or a semi-fitted pinwale corduroy or shantung skirt in a style well proportioned for this type of figure is worth considering. Keep colors for skirts and pants dark to minimize bulk in the hip area. Balance the body with light or bright colors for blouses, tops, and sweaters.

The figure with a large bust and narrow hips will look good in medium-thick or thick fabrics for skirts, and thin fabrics for blouses and tops. An interesting outfit could consist of a velveteen skirt with a crepe overblouse, bringing the top-heavy body into scale. As you consider various colors at the fabric store, be sure to try a variety of fabrics with different surface treatments for the narrow part of your body. You may be pleasantly surprised by how well thick and thin fabrics in the same color, or in harmonizing shades, work together for your figure.

Women with square or round figures should look for fabrics in solid colors that are flat-surfaced or have textures that lead the eye from head to toe, not horizontally. Plain doubleknits and singleknits, other vertical ribs or textures, gabardine and twill with their diagonal weaves, and some of the thinnest pinwale corduroys will all make complementary garments. Jumpers, dresses, coats, and suits with skirts or pants in one solid color (none too bright), with contrasting accents or accessories, are wise choices. Be sure to drape the fabric over your body in the store to make certain that it will work for you. You may be able to mix plainweave and textured fabrics of one color, or harmonizing shades for separates, if the pattern style is right for you.

There are many possibilities in selecting solid colors and textures. Remember to use the fabric's thickness and design in the most flattering way you can. Review the color chapter, if necessary, as you try on new and exciting solid-color fabric and different fabric textures.

Fabric Designs

The artistry used to add another dimension to fabric is unlimited—from tiny all-over prints to bold, accentuating designs—each individual feature can help create a fashionable garment.

Stripes

There are three types of stripes to be considered: lengthwise, crosswise, and diagonal.

Lengthwise stripes are generally flattering to the large woman. The only ones you should steer clear of are broad, bold, thick stripes that may make you look as if you are wearing a flag or awning.

Crosswise stripes are sometimes considered flattering for the large woman when done as narrow bands of muted shades or tints. You may be able to use them successfully if you wish to balance broad hips or large thighs with a contrasting crosswise-striped top combined with a solid-color skirt or pants. For the large-busted woman, narrow crosswise stripes used for a skirt or pants with a solid-color top may be just the outfit to balance the figure.

Most home sewers tend to stay away from *diagonal stripes* because they are difficult to match at seams. However, when used for a plain A-line shift or skimmer, they can flatter an ample figure. Staying with garments with few seams (none in center-front, for example) and narrow, diagonal stripes will minimize obvious matching problems.

Plaids and Checks

Careful selection is the key when using plaids and checks for your fashions.

Plaids come in many styles, from tiny, continuous patterns to large, wide bands running down and across the fabric. They may be bright and bold or softly tinted, even (the same pattern horizontally as vertically) or uneven (different patterns in both directions). Whatever type you are considering, make sure it will complement your figure. Plaids with small patterns or with the biggest bands running lengthwise are the best choices. If you feel plaids are too overwhelming for an entire outfit, try a softly toned plaid jacket, vest, or top combined with a solid skirt or pants. Top-heavy and bottom-heavy figures can use plaids on the smaller part of the body, with solid coordinating colors on the larger part for a balanced look.

Checks do not require as much consideration as plaids, but you must look at the size of the check before you buy. Small checks, ⅛ inch to ½ inch, are usually suitable for everyone. The larger the check, the less likely it will be flattering to your figure, especially if used over the largest area of your body.

Prints

These fabrics seem to come in more patterns than there are stars in the sky. Florals, geometrics, dots, novelty, juvenile, all-over designs, panels, and border prints are all fascinating to look at and consider. The fabric manufacturing process has become so sophisticated with computer-controlled machinery that almost anything can be printed on yard goods.

Your main concern will be to select a print that will flatter you. Small design motifs are not usually a problem if the color is right; it will be the large-scale print that you must carefully evaluate.

Florals and geometrics have so many beautiful colors it almost seems impossible to choose one. Avoid dominating splashes of color or large design motifs that may accent your figure flaws (a large blossom right in the middle of a large bust, for example), or lead the eye across the body, giving an illusion of greater girth. Drape the fabric over your body right there in the store to check before making a purchase.

Dots have long been a favorite, classic fabric design. Small polka dots are a welcome addition to any wardrobe. But always test large or multicolored dots carefully in front of the store mirror before you buy.

Novelty and juvenile prints usually have a predominantly colored figure or character that must be evaluated carefully in relation to your figure. You may want to use this type of fabric as an accent or for a separate top, overblouse, or jacket. Cartoon-type characters on fabric are no longer the singular domain of small fry, and these prints can make colorful additions to your sportswear wardrobe. Just remember to test how these fabrics look on your body. Stay away from those that may emphasize problem figure areas, or those that make you look lumpy or bulky.

Fabrics with all-over designs usually have almost identical motifs without a "top" or "bottom" to the design. For example, in a floral design, flowers will be arranged with some running in opposite directions to others. The pattern pieces may be placed on the fabric running in either direction along the grain. This means that as you face the fabric on the table, the top of the sleeve pattern could point to the right, while the top of the bodice pattern could be pointing to the left (*without nap* is the term used on the instruction sheet for this kind of layout). Testing the fabric for its suitability to you is the key here, for your time and money are valuable.

One-way designs have the motifs going in only one direction on the length of the fabric. Stems of flowers are all pointing in the same direction, or little cars may be running parallel to each other in the same direction. Whatever the design, pattern pieces must all be cut out in the same direction, using a *with nap* layout on your pattern instruction sheet. One-way designs may lead the eye across the figure or up and down, so be sure this type of fabric will not disturb the balance or proportion of the garment you plan to sew. Again, test the fabric carefully in front of a store mirror before making a final decision.

Border prints have a distinctive design, usually printed or woven in along one selvage. The border may be quite pronounced, or it may be subtle and flowing. The borders are most often used at the hem of a dress or skirt. Such dresses or skirts may be fitted, semifitted, slightly-fitted, or loosely-fitted, but should have straight side seams where the border will fall. Occasionally, borders are used for yokes or at the bottom of a long, straight, or flared, uncuffed sleeve. Skirts using border prints may be pleated or gathered. Recently, one pattern company introduced a quarter-circle skirt with a border print shown cascading down one side, a very pretty effect. Both the style—a vertical design—and the fabric are flattering to the full-figured woman. Let your designer instincts take over when you see an attractive border print. Use it down one side of a dress, or have two borders meet, both vertical, at the center-front, with a zipper closing. The right border print will create an unusual garment, and the up and down design lines will be very figure flattering.

Panels characteristically repeat a design or show a continuous picture or design. They are most often created for wall hangings or household accessories, such as pillows and cushions. Smaller panels can be used for T-shirts, blouses, and pajama fronts that pull over the head or close in the back. You can use the panel for the back of a jacket or blouse. This type of fabric is purchased by the panel, not by the yard, so put your designing talents to work. Create your own one-of-a-kind garment or accessory, such as a hostess skirt (made entirely of one large or many small panels), tote bags, or use small panels as appliqués on other garments.

Fabric printed with small panels can be used to make figure-flattering garments. Find one that has a softly shaded border around a rectangle and a muted or other allover print inside each panel. Lay out the pattern pieces so the borders of the panels go down the center-front and center-back of the dress, creating a vertical line that projects a more slender image. Remember to match the panel borders at side seams and any center seams. While these prints will add some sparkle to your wardrobe, make sure a motif does not emphasize problem parts of your body instead of camouflaging them.

Fabric Comfort and Care Requirements

1. Will the fabric be comfortable to wear? Run your hands over both the right and wrong sides of the fabric. Rub the wrong side on your cheek and on an arm. Does it scratch or make you feel itchy, or does it feel smooth and pleasant? Does it have a loopy surface that will catch jewelry or other items you wear and carry? Does it have openings and holes that will reveal undergarments, requiring a special slip? Also, check fiber content. Sometimes natural fibers are preferable to synthetics because they allow the skin to breathe. This is especially important in warm weather, when a pure cotton dress will be much cooler than a polyester or nylon garment. Because of the in-

ability of synthetics to let air pass freely through the fabric, these materials are hot and can chafe and irritate sensitive skins. Remember, you will be wearing your newly sewn garment for a long time, and you should enjoy the feel of the fabric next to your bare skin and be comfortable in it.

2. What type of care is required? Look at the fabric hang tag or the label at the end of the cardboard bolt to see the recommended care of the fabric and its fiber content. Softer fabrics may contain rayon and acetate blends together with natural or other synthetic fibers. These rayon and acetate fibers often shrink a good deal more than pure cottons or polyesters when washed and dried in the dryer, so take note. If you are planning a washable garment, preshrink the fabric: soak it in water for about one-half hour; then dry it in the same way you will dry the finished garment. Some of the newest fabrics, especially knits, may shrink so much that you may need some extra yardage to compensate.

Be sure to find out the precise way to care for your fabric. When it says *drip dry*, it will shrink in the heat of a hot dryer, so pay attention. Machine wash does not always mean machine dry.

To see how much the fabric wrinkles, and to check for a permanent-press finish, make a ball of the fabric and squeeze. Release the fabric and see how long it takes for the wrinkles to disappear. If they immediately vanish, little or no ironing will be needed. Many new

fashions and patterns are designed for fabrics that require some ironing, so be aware of these properties when making your final fabric selection.

Fabric Quality and Workmanship

1. Will the quality be suitable? For a one-time glamorous or special occasion, you need not be too concerned with the longevity of your fabric. But, for those classic wardrobe items that must last several seasons, you should get durable, quality material. Otherwise, why spend the time sewing? Durability does not mean that the fabric must be thick or heavy. For example, a quality voile is a sheer, lightweight fabric that can withstand many wearings, as will a good, fairly lightweight shantung. The strength, blend, and finishing of the fibers help to make a longer-lasting garment.

Look for a firm weave or knit in both soft and crisp fabrics. Scratch the fabric to see if the yarns or threads shift. Poorly constructed fabric will wear out quickly when it rubs over the roundness of your body.

Look for weak or thin spots or other imperfections. Hold the fabric up to a light or window to check for thick and thin areas. Fabrics with defects like these will wear out much too soon.

Rub the fabric between your hands. If a powdery residue appears, and the fabric goes soft or limp, put it back. It was probably treated with what is called *sizing*, a chemical meant to give the fabric an appearance of body. Sizing is often used to mask fabric of inferior quality. The sizing usually washes out, leaving you with a limp, cheap-looking garment.

Be sure to examine both right and wrong sides of the fabric before it is cut. Yard goods are made on fast-moving machines, and for this reason it is very hard to maintain a tight quality control. Look for runs, pulls, skipped weaves or stitches, knots and lumps that have been printed over, soil marks, holes, and misprints. You do not want to pay top-dollar for fabric that has even minor imperfections. But, after careful examination, if you decide you can work around a small flaw, most reputable shopkeepers will allow you an extra quarter of a yard or more as compensation. Ask for this if it is not offered and you really want the fabric. When expensive fabric is involved, many shops will allow you to spread out the fabric and do a rough layout with your pattern pieces to make sure you can avoid imperfections when cutting out the garment. The extra time spent doing this will be worth it if you have already spent a lot of time finding the ideal fabric for your pattern. You certainly do not want to find out you cannot work around problem areas *after* you have started cutting!

2. Is the fabric on the straight grain? This means that the weave, or knit, is not distorted in any way. There are three ways the fabric can be off-grain: it can be woven or knitted off-grain; it can be printed off-grain; or it can have a permanent-press finish, applied off-grain, making it both permanently pressed and permanently off-grain. Straight-grain fabrics should have the lengthwise threads on wovens, or the rib on knits, parallel to the selvage edge. The crosswise threads on wovens or the courses of the knits would be at right angles to the selvage.

Off-grain woven and knitted fabrics will not drape properly, no matter how hard you try. When the garment is worn, each half of the garment will hang differently.

Avoid off-grain fabric, or if it is the last of a kind and you really want it, try to straighten the grain before you cut. Pull on the fabric diagonally, on the bias grain, in the direction that the grain needs to be straightened. With natural fabrics— cottons, woolens, linens and silks— the grain is usually straightened without too much effort. But on synthetics and permanent-press fabrics, you may not have much success, so think twice before buying off-grain fabric.

3. Is the fabric's color true? Open the fabric and examine it in full light. Check both sides to make sure the color is true and even from selvage to selvage in the full length you plan to purchase. Also, if the fabric is folded and wrapped on a bolt, check the fold to see that it is not faded or soiled. Rub the fabric between your hands to make certain that the color does not come off on your skin. Powdery color residue is an indication that the dyeing process or fabric finishing was inferior. During wear, this dye will rub off and discolor your skin and undergarments. When laundered, the dye will run and perhaps discolor other garments in the same washload.

High-speed fabric printing and dyeing processes do not allow for close quality control, so you must be your own fabric inspector. Solid colors, prints, plaids, stripes, and geometrics should be checked for irregularities and off-printing. Light spots, streaks, and tiny folds may occur during the printing and dyeing, and you would not want these flaws appearing in your finished garment. Color imperfections will never help to make a quality garment, so be aware, and keep your eyes open.

Special Fabrics

There are some exciting and distinctive fabrics, each with their own personality, that you may want to wear. Consider each type carefully—each has special handling requirements—before selecting one for that particular garment you want to sew.

Napped Fabrics

These fabrics reflect light in one direction down their length and absorb it in the other direction, creating a brightness, or richer look in one direction and a dullness, or softer look, in the other. To find out if your fabric has a nap, stand in a well-lighted spot. Drape one end over your body, then reverse the fabric, to see which direction reflects light and appears brigher. All pattern pieces must be cut out going in the same direction, otherwise your garment sections will appear to be different colors. If your pattern does not have a *with nap* layout, and you are considering a napped fabric, check the instruction sheet to see how many of the main pattern pieces are laid out in the same direction. Most likely you will need to purchase additional yardage to create the *with nap*, or one-way, layout. How much extra yardage you will need will depend on how much the given pattern layout will have to be changed.

Press seams and construction details in napped fabrics over a needle board or over scraps of the same fabric, face sides together. Or, pad your ironing board with several layers of toweling to avoid crushing the nap while you press.

The most familiar napped fabrics are corduroy, velvet, velveteen, and velour. Others that may have to be treated as napped fabrics because of their shiny surface are satin, some polished cottons, and chintz. Brushed fabrics—knits, woolens, blends, etc.—should also be treated as napped fabrics.

Sheers and Laces

These lovely fabrics deserve a place in your wardrobe, too. I recommend that you underline the garment shell so you have smooth, unbroken lines that will show off the fabric but not any areas of your body to a disadvantage. Sleeves do not need to be underlined. You can take advantage of fabric sheerness by making a fancy, loose jacket or special fashion accessory such as a poncho or stole, using French seams and narrow hems, for an added touch of glamor to a special ensemble. CAUTION: Give yourself a little more wearing ease for garments made of these delicate fabrics.

Satin

These slippery beauties make elegant blouses, tops, dresses, and even skirts or pants when the fabric's thickness and color are selected with care. Satins are seen now as daytime fabrics, too, and you will probably enjoy at least one garment made in this special fabric. Most woven and knitted satins should be handled as napped fabrics, and you will need a little more wearing ease so the seams will not pull out. If the fabric slides around on your table when you are laying

out the pattern, pin the satin to an old sheet to keep it in place during cutting. Be careful when pressing these fabrics. Test press first, and use a press cloth on the wrong side of the satin.

Crepe

No matter what type of crepe garment you make, it will feel elegant on your skin and, of course, drape beautifully. Color and thickness are your main concerns when selecting a crepe. Why not pick a luxurious satin-back crepe for a shirtdress, coatdress, or a two-piece tailored dress. Use the satin side for the collar, lapels, covered buttons, and belt for the kind of haute couture finish that designers employ.

If you have trouble with skipped stitches, use a fine needle (no. 9 or 11) and strips of tissue paper over and under the seamlines. Long staple polyester thread may help—so can loosening the thread tension on your machine. Be careful not to stretch the cut edges—you may want to staystitch to be sure—as you sew, or you may end up with wobbly seams. Be sure to allow enough wearing ease so the fabric can drape gracefully over your figure.

6

Making Patterns Work for You

If you are truly interested in being fashionably dressed and having superbly-fitting clothes, take the time to learn how it can happen with the help of well-known commercial patterns. The commercial pattern companies also publish books and leaflets that show how to make patterns fit. If you are unsure about how to get the most out of your patterns, these publications should help. You may also want to try a new pattern for the extra-large-size woman called *Sew Elegant: For the Woman Fashion Forgets.* It has sixteen versions in sizes 16 to 60, and is manufactured by a Los Angeles company. (These patterns are available through NAAFA.).

As we move into pattern variations, just remember never to be afraid to experiment. Think of your pattern tissue as a tool that you can use to get the desired effect. The sometimes limited selections presented by commercial pattern companies can be adapted to make many different-looking garments. Do not be afraid to change a neckline, add a pleat, or make any other style change to lend more variety to your clothes. You can also convert skirts and pants with waistbands to garments with elasticized waists.

Pattern Adjustments and Alterations

You are a unique, one-of-a-kind figure. All women are. Since commercial patterns are made to standardized measurements, the chances of a perfect pattern fit are not great. It is no one's fault. The pattern companies have to start somewhere with their sizing. So do you, which is why you took all those measurements listed in chapter 3. Pattern adjustments are vital to a good fit. After you learn how to do the ones you need, they will easily become part of your sewing routine.

You may need to make a test garment first to make sure the style, pattern alterations, balance, and proportions are right. Use any firmly woven fabric, even the usable parts of an old sheet. Sew the garment shell and the sleeves together with machine basting (these stitches can be ripped out easily), so you can use the fitted pieces as a pattern if necessary.

Before you adjust the next pattern, think about the last outfit you made. How well did it fit? Was it balanced on your figure? Many times all that is needed is a raised or lowered waist, seam, or hem, or a little more circumference in the fabric so it drapes fluidly over the body. Usually, the more fitted the style the more personalized adjustments you will need.

There are certain times when you may want to reduce style ease by omitting part of your required hip adjustment. This is an acceptable procedure if you have ample room at the waist for the garment to hang well on your figure. The measurements you took in chapter 3, compared to those on the pattern envelope for hips, let you know how much, if any, reduction in style ease can be made.

Hip and Waist Changes

For most figure types, increases are needed. I recommend that you slash skirt patterns from hem to waist, and one-piece dresses from hem to within several inches of the bust dart and at a right angle to the side seamline (figure 6–1). Adjust front and back pieces in the same manner. Add one-fourth of the total amount needed to each pattern piece, front and back, since these pieces each represent only one-quarter of the garment. Spread the pieces over tissue or other paper. Check for accuracy and then tape permanently in place.

After the garment has been cut out, baste in existing darts and try on the garment. If needed, make deeper darts, add another one, or ease the skirt to fit the waistband or bodice. For a one-piece dress, retain the side seamline shape, smoothing out the cutting lines at the waist.

Slash a skirt or pants waistband apart at side-seam markings. Spread the waistband apart over paper, leaving one-half the total amount of space needed at each side, and tape to the paper.

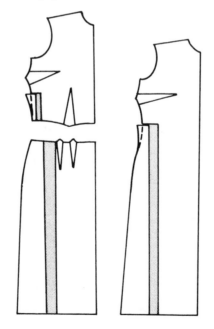

Figure 6–1

Large-Bust Changes

There are many complex ways to adjust patterns for a large bust, but in most cases it can be made quite easy. Simply split the bodice front or blouse front up through the middle of the shoulder seam (figure 6–2). Place pieces over tissue or other paper. Spread pieces apart, leaving one-half the total amount of space needed between them (pattern represents half the garment—the front, cut on a double layer of fabric—and you do not make bust alterations to the back). Check for accuracy and then tape permanently in place.

To make the garment fit at shoulders and waist, make several narrow tucks, darts, or add gathers. (See the Narrow Shoulders alteration in chapter 9.)

If you want to add an inch or less to the bust, extend the front underarm seamline outward one-half the amount needed. Do the same on the sleeve at the front underarm seamline. Draw new seamlines downward on each piece, tapering back to the original seamline at front waist and at the lower edge of the sleeve.

Sleeve Changes

A fitted sleeve must have ample wearing ease to be comfortable and look good. To enlarge sleeves (figure 6–3), trace the upper edge of the sleeve onto a piece of paper. Place the pattern on tissue or other paper. Slash pattern up the center along the grainline, and spread the pieces apart, leaving the full amount of space needed between them. Secure with tape. Most sleeves will not need any adjustments at the lower edge when the sleeve has been enlarged.

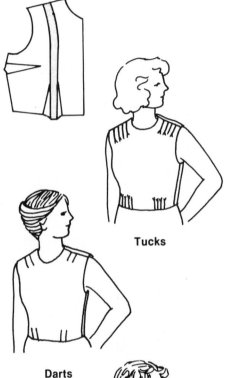

Tucks

Darts

Shirring

Figure 6-2

For a set-in sleeve, redraw the sleeve cap so it will be in the original shape. Mark the center of the sleeve cap so you can match it to the shoulder seam. Lower the underarm curve on front and back bodice pattern pieces, between the notches, about ¼ inch for every inch you added to the sleeve width. After the underarm seam is stitched, add another ease thread between the notches and across the underarm seam so any excess fabric may be eased to fit the bodice (1).

For a raglan sleeve, redraw the top to fit the original shape, making a slightly deeper dart. After the underarm seam is stitched, add an ease thread between the notches and across the underarm seam so any excess fabric may be eased to fit the bodice (2).

For both types of long sleeves without a cuff, make two narrow darts at the lower sides (after the seam is stitched, center the seam in the middle and make darts along the side folds). Complete sleeve hem as directed by your pattern (3).

Pants Changes

Most large women arrive at a pants pattern that fits well, then never use another style of pattern. If you do this, how about being a little more daring? Try pants that have tiny pleats instead of darts, or a new, tailored style. If your favorite pants pattern has been adjusted to fit you well, place it underneath the new-style pattern pieces. It will be obvious where any changes will be needed—crotch length, waist, hips—and you will know if the new style will have the same wearing ease or more over the hips. Make changes as needed at the side seams.

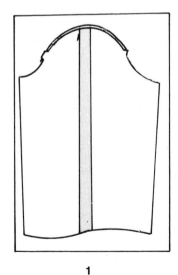

1

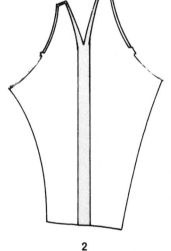

2

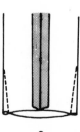

3

Figure 6-3

Muslin Fitting Pattern: The best way to get a perfect-fitting pair of pants is to work out all the problems in muslin. Make any obvious alterations in your pattern and cut it out of muslin or any other firm, woven fabric, such as an old sheet. Transfer all seamlines and markings, including grainlines, to the *right* side of the fabric with a tracing wheel and dressmaker's carbon paper. This will allow you to see the exact placement of the darts and the straight grain of the fabric as it drapes (or does not drape) over your body. Stitch the pants with machine basting for easier alterations. Add any additional fabric at the sides, or take in the pants until they hang smoothly, with the marked grainlines perpendicular to the floor. NOTE: When dealing with extreme disproportions, you may want to use a pants fitting pattern sold by the commercial pattern companies, that comes with instructions for personalized fitting.

When the muslin pants fit to your satisfaction, take them apart, making sure there is a ⅝-inch seam allowance on all seams. Use the muslin pieces as a pattern to make perfect-fitting pants. When you see another pants style you want to try, it is easy to adjust the paper pattern by laying your muslin pattern pieces under it. Enlarge and decrease each new pattern piece as indicated by your muslin, being careful not to distort the new style lines.

You can also adjust your favorite pants pattern to taper the legs, as sometimes pants that hang straight down from the hips are too wide, especially for shorter women. You will need to make new cutting lines (figure 6–4). Take an equal amount from the inseam and side seams, being careful not to make the pants too tight at the knee. Draw in new lines from the hem to the crotch at the inseam and to the full hips at the side seam.

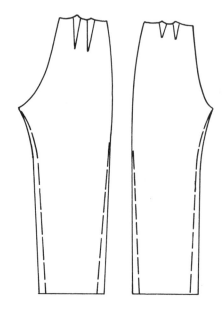

Figure 6–4

Pattern Variations

Now is the time to become your own designer. Make those patterns work for you: mix and match sleeves, necklines, and other style features. You know which is your best skirt and bodice style, so go ahead and make a switch—put the bodice of one pattern with the skirt of another (as long as they have the same waist-seam location). Or, add shirt sleeves to a classic top for a change of style. A word of caution, however. Be sure to use the same brand of pattern when interchanging pieces (a Butterick with a Butterick, etc.). Each company has its own unique grading techniques for drafting patterns. For example, each pattern company makes sleeves that fit precisely into their armholes, but will not fit another company's. The same is true of necklines and waist seams. But do not be afraid to try changing patterns around. Explore the many possibilities for pattern variations on the following pages. You may find yourself doing many things with patterns that you never thought of before.

A Dress into a Jumper

It is quite easy to transform a dress into a jumper worn with a blouse underneath. Use a dress pattern that has no waistline seam, or one that has a lot of vertical lines.

To make the transformation (figure 6–5), add ¼ inch to each side seam of the garment front, back, and armhole facings, if you have them. To enlarge the armholes, make a new cutting line ⅝ inch below the original cutting line on both armhole and armhole facings, tapering back to the original cutting line at the notches. Add ⅝ inch to the outer curve of the facing in the same way. Stitch armhole and side seams, using a ⅝-inch seam allowance.

If the dress pattern has no armhole facings, trace new front and back (lowered) armhole cutting lines. Trace shoulder and side-seam cutting lines away from the armhole seam for 2½ inches. Connect the ends of the traced lines in a smooth curve to create armhole facings that are 2½ inches wide.

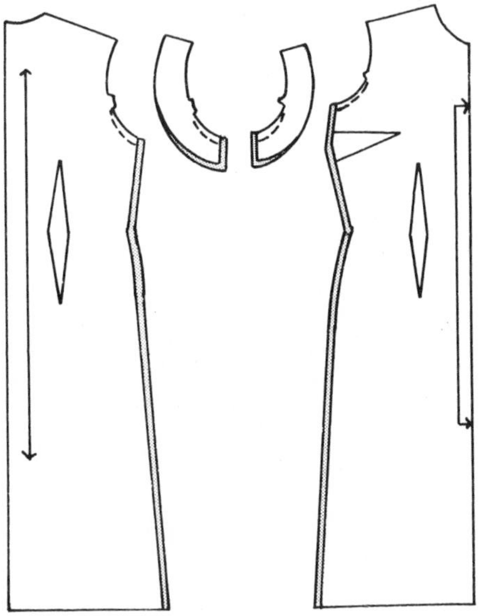

the neckline to your pattern, adding a ⅝-inch seam allowance. Make a facing to match the new neckline. Make the facing about 3 inches wide, tracing it from the neckline between shoulder and center-front. Using a ruler, draw in about one inch at a time of the facing's outer edge, then shape the edge into a smooth line (figure 6–6). For a

lowered, round neckline (1) you may find that tracing around a saucer or small plate helps you to get a smooth facing line. The V-neck (2) is the easiest to make and it can be as high or deep as you like. U-necklines (3) are really softened square necklines and are very flattering. Simply draw in a square and round off the corners.

Figure 6–5

Necklines

If you do not have the neckline you want in your pattern collection, you can make your own in your most flattering style. Select a pattern you know fits well and cut out a whole new bodice front from paper. Draw in the new neckline and cut out along the marking. To check how the neckline will look, hold the test pattern over yourself to see if it is satisfactory. Transfer

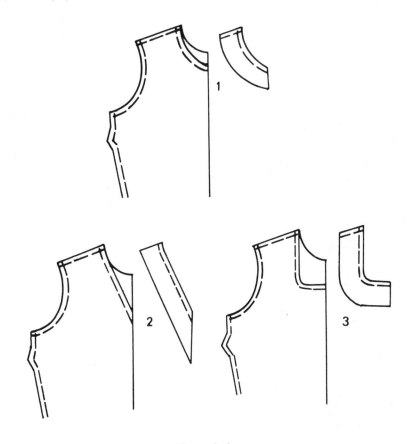

Figure 6–6

Sleeves

There are several ways you can add interest to sleeves, changing them from plain, straight, fitted, or shirt-type styles into unique designs.

To add a pleat to a long sleeve (figure 6–7), split the pattern through its center along the grainline. Add 4 inches (1). Additional yardage may be required. After sleeve has been cut from fabric, fold each sleeve, right sides together, along the center of the pleat allowance. Pin. Machine-baste 2 inches from fold (2). Pleat may be stitched from wrist to elbow, or only at the elbow on the right side, for about 2 inches (5). Center pleat fabric over basted (and stitched) line, and press flat (4). Complete sleeve as directed by your pattern. Remove basting (6).

To add a pleat to a short sleeve (figure 6–8), split the pattern through the center, along the grainline, and add 4 inches (1). Additional yardage may be required. After the sleeve has been cut out, fold each sleeve, right sides together, along the center of the pleat allowance. Pin, and machine-baste 2 inches from the fold (2). Pleat may hang free or may be stitched 1½ inches above the hemline down to the lower edge (3). Center the pleat fabric over the basted (and stitched) seam and press flat (4). To reduce bulk on the stitched version, trim away excess pleat fabric along the hemline to within ½ inch of the stitching (5). Complete sleeve as directed by pattern. Remove basting from the free-hanging pleat before hemming (6).

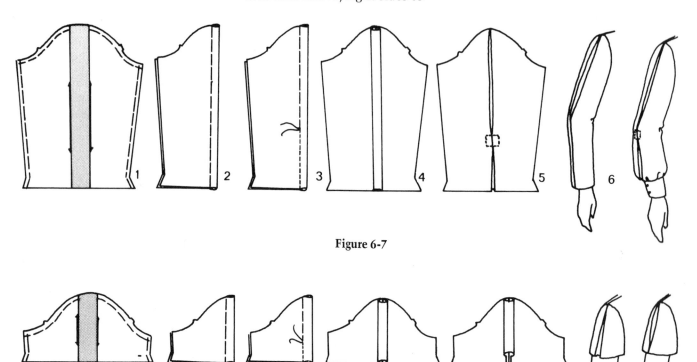

Figure 6-7

Figure 6-8

To add gathers to a short sleeve (figure 6-9), split the pattern through the center along the grainline and add 4 inches (1). Additional yardage may be required. After sleeve has been cut out, add two rows of gathering threads on the sleeve cap between the notches (2). Finish lower edge of sleeve with a ⅜-inch casing, adding in ¼-inch wide elastic (3). Or, make a square opening with a tie closure (4). (You will find these procedures in chapter 7, Openings with Ties.)

Jackets

There are several things you can do to change a jacket style—adding vents or a center-back pleat. You can also use your favorite blouse pattern and turn it into a jacket.

To add vents to side seams, use a square or curved shape (figure 6-10). Make a dot 4 to 5 inches above the jacket hemline, on the seamline (1). Add the same amount outward to the side seam below the dot as is used for the hem allowance. For a curved opening, trace around a saucer or small plate (2). Stitch side seams, leaving open below the dot. Press seam open and side opening edges to the inside along original seamlines. Turn up the hem and press. Finish raw edges of hem and vents as your fabric requires. Fold in excess and miter corners for square vents (3). For curved vents, add a row of ease stitching ¼ inch from the upper edge. Adjust the ease to fit the curve smoothly. Machine-stitch or hand-sew hem in place.

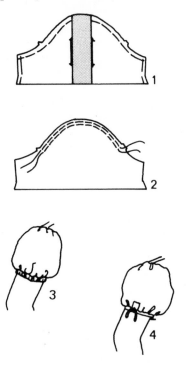

Figure 6-9:

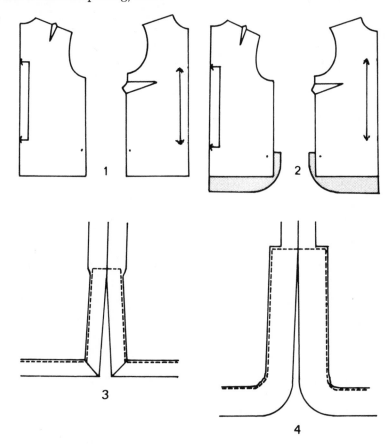

Figure 6-10

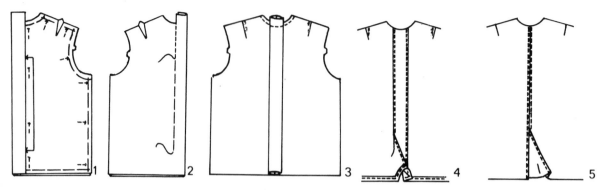

Figure 6-11

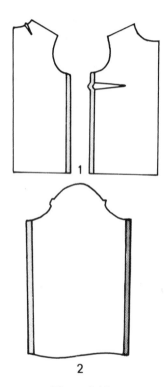

Figure 6-12

To add a center-back pleat (figure 6–11), place center-back foldline 3 inches away from the fabric fold when laying out the pattern. Additional yardage may be required. Extend the pleat fabric up, even with the shoulders (1). Stitch down about 4 inches below neck edge, and 3 inches in from fabric fold. Machine-baste below stitching to hem edge (2). Center pleat fabric over jacket and press flat to within 6 inches of the hem edge. Machine-baste neck edges together through all thicknesses and trim pleat to fit neck curve (3).

After jacket is hemmed, press pleat flat. On the inside of the jacket, stitch ⅛ inch from each inner pleat fold, continuing over the hem (4) and keeping front free. On the outside, stitch ⅛ inch from each pleat fold, from hem to as far up as possible, keeping back free (5).

Transforming a blouse pattern into a jacket (figure 6–12) requires simple changes. Add ½ inch to both back and front pattern pieces at the side seams (1), and at both underarm sleeve seam edges (2). NOTE: For medium- to heavyweight or thick fabrics, add ½ inch to the center-back of the collar and garment pattern pieces if you want to close the top button. Thicker fabric will create bulk along the collar and jacket neck seam, making it too small if these adjustments are not made. Cuffs may need an additional ½ inch also.

Skirt Changes

Skirt changes are another easy way to vary patterns. If you have a firm figure, and can wear straight or slightly A-line skirts, you can add the vents as shown for jackets, to side and center seams.

Gathers: You may want to modify your favorite straight or A-line skirt with 2 to 3 inches of soft gathers on each side of the center-front (figure 6–13), in place of darts. Slash the pattern front (and back, if desired) parallel to the grainline through or between darts. Spread the pattern apart 2 to 3 inches over paper. Check for accuracy and tape in place. This will increase the skirt circumference up to 12 inches, so be very conservative as you proceed. Your fabric is most important (1). It should be fairly soft and drape well.

After the skirt is cut out, clip-mark the waist at outermost dart stitching lines. Add two sets of gathering threads between markings. Adjust gathers so skirt will fit bodice or waistband (2).

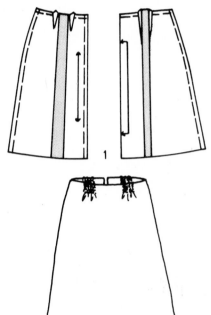

Figure 6-13

Pleats: To make center-front and/or center-back pleats in a skirt (figure 6–14), add 6 to 8 inches at the center-front and/or center-back (1). Additional yardage may be required. After skirt pieces have been cut out, stitch extended center-back seam and insert zipper. Now machine-baste along the original seamline or foldline (2).

For pressed pleats, center pleat fabric over basting and press flat to within 6 inches of lower edge. For a center-back pleat, align basting with center of zipper and stitch over previous zipper stitching through all thicknesses (3). For a center-front pleat, on the outside, stitch ¼ inch

from each side of the basting to about $7\frac{5}{8}$ inches below waist seam, as shown (4), pivoting stitching across pleat. Complete skirt as usual, removing pleat basting threads before hemming. Press pleat across hem. Edgestitch inside pleat folds within the hem allowance for a permanent crease.

For unpressed pleats, after zipper is inserted, center pleat fabric over basting. Press upper edges for about 2 inches below the waist. Steam remainder of pleat and pat flat with your hands. Allow fabric to air dry. Baste upper edges together and remove basting (5). Complete skirt.

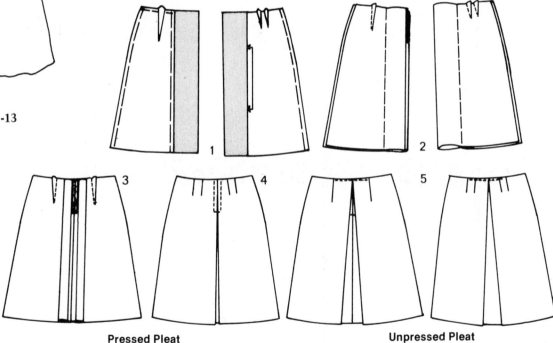

Pressed Pleat   Unpressed Pleat

Figure 6-14:

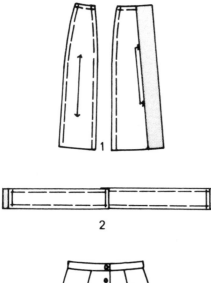

2

3

Figure 6-15

Button Front: Turn your favorite back-zippered skirt into an easy-on, front-buttoned style (figure 6–15). For ½-inch to ⅝-inch buttons or hammer-on snaps, add 4 inches to the center-front fold. One inch is for an extension so your skirt will have an overlap of 2 inches (one on each side), and 3 inches for a self-facing (1). Lap waistband pattern piece ends, matching center-back markings. Pin. Cut apart along center-front markings and add 1-⅝ inches to each end for the extension and a seam allowance (2). Add interfacing to the 3-inch facing on both right and left sides. When skirt is completed, add as many buttons or snaps as desired (3).

Elasticized or Drawstring Waist

A skirt or pants with an elasticized or drawstring waist is a must for many large women. Water retention is often a problem, causing as much as a five-pound variation in weight during one day. When this happens, it is impossible to tolerate anything tight, especially around the waist.

To adapt the pattern for an expanding waist (figure 6–16), you must enlarge the waistline so it will be easy to slip into the garment. The zipper is eliminated, as are any darts. Add twice the width of elastic or drawstring, plus ½ inch to the top of the pattern for a turned-under edge. For example, if you were using 1-inch-wide elastic, you would add 2-½ inches to the top of the pattern. Extend side seamlines straight up above the waist from the hip. Sew all seams. Follow directions in chapter 7 for an elasticized or drawstring casing.

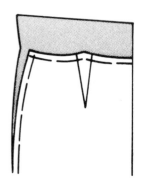

Figure 6-16

7

Sewing Tips

There are some special insider tips that will help you sew more attractive clothes for your unique figure. The sewing tips on the following pages are meant to stimulate your creativity, perhaps even to the extent that you will come up with some new ideas of your own. These suggestions will enable you to add more variety to your wardrobe, and be very attractively dressed—as a result of your own fashion efforts.

Belts that Minimize

The worst problem the large woman has with belts is that they so often roll up into a long tube and become unattractive. When you have a definite waistline, and the pattern calls for a belt, you should always use a stiff, inner belting. Find a shop that sells it by the yard so you will not have to worry about piecing it, as is sometimes necessary when purchased precut in a package. Remember a 1- to 1½-

inch-wide belt will look best. Use this belting to interface waistbands of skirts and pants, too, if you have problems with curling there as well.

Tie Belt

To stiffen a tie belt, cut a piece of stiff belting 3 inches less than your waist measurement. Round off the ends. Cut a fabric strip the length recommended for your pattern, and twice as wide as the belting, plus ½ inch for two, ¼-inch seam allowances. Wrap fabric over the belting, right sides together (figure 7–1). Using a zipper foot, stitch close to belting, leaving an opening at the center of the belt. Remove belting and stitch the ends shut (2). Turn belt right side out and press. Insert belting into opening, centering it in tie belt. Slipstitch opening shut. Make sure belt fabric is taut over belting and stitch along curved ends through all thicknesses to hold belting in place (3).

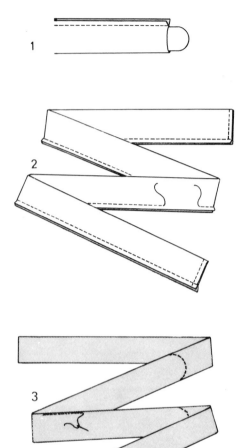

as the belting, plus ½ inch for two, ¼-inch seam allowances. One end of the belting may be shaped into a point. Wrap fabric over the belting, right sides on the inside. Using a zipper foot, stitch close to belting (1). Bring seam to center of belting and press seam open with tip of iron, never resting iron on belt edges. Make sure fabric extends over the shaped end of belting, and stitch end. Trim away excess fabric (2). Remove belting and turn belt right side out. Insert shaped end of belting into open end of belt. Make sure fabric is taut on belting. Slip

the open end of belt over the buckle bar and mark belt where the prong will go through (3). Tuck remaining raw end to the inside and stitch in place through all thicknesses (4).

To make a hole for the prong, stitch a rectangle at marking, ¼-inch wide and 1-inch long, as shown. Slash through all thicknesses between stitching (5). Slip prong into the hole and fold belt end over the bar; sew end in place by hand or machine. Apply metal eyelets at opposite end according to the eyelet manufacturer's directions (6).

Figure 7-1

Belt with Prong Buckle

For this type of belt, use stiff belting the length of your waist measurement, plus 7 inches.

To make belt (figure 7–2), cut a fabric strip the length of the belting plus ½ inch for two, ¼-inch end-seam allowances, and twice as wide

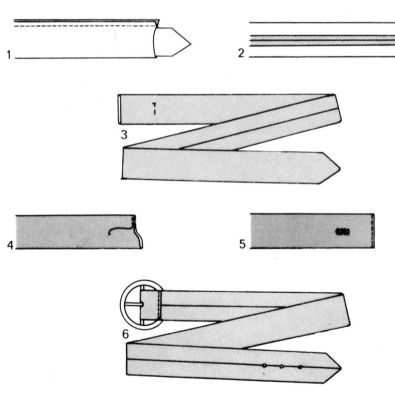

Figure 7-2

Belt with Clasp Buckle

For a belt with a clasp buckle, use stiff belting for your waist measurement, plus 3 inches for a 1½-inch extension at each end of the belt, so it will fit over the clasp bars. In most cases this length is adequate, but the size of the buckle will determine if you need a longer or shorter extension.

To make belt and insert belting, follow figure 7–2, steps one and two for a prong buckle. Tuck in raw ends and stitch in same manner as step four for a prong buckle. Try on belt (figure 7–3), and mark belt where it goes over the clasp bars (1). Sew ends in place by hand or machine (2).

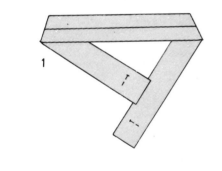

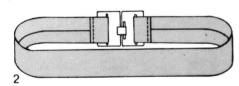

Figure 7-3

Casings

There is nothing like an elasticized or drawstring casing on a sleeve or at the waist to provide added comfort for the ample figure. Casings control garment fullness, add a perky fashion feature, and allow for body expansion in women who have a water-retention problem.

When adding a casing to the lower edge of a blouse or jacket, allow an extra inch of length, if possible, in the body of the garment for *blousing*, so the fabric can gather gracefully along the elastic or drawstring.

Elasticized Casings

Select soft, densely woven or braided elastic that will not become narrower as you stretch it. Some elastics will roll inside the casing as the garment is worn, so look for nonroll elastics that are specifically designed to hold their shape at the waistline.

Plain casings, cut-in-one with the garment, are easy to add to a sleeve or blouse pattern. When there is a ⅝-inch seam allowance on the bottom edge where you would like to add a casing, you can use a ¼-inch-wide elastic without changing the pattern. Do not be alarmed if the garment's curved edge causes puckers in the casing after you have turned up the edge. When the elastic is inserted, the puckers will disappear in the gathers.

If there is a hem allowance on the pattern, you may simply choose an elastic width that will accommodate the entire hem allowance if it is turned up into a casing; or trim the excess hem allowance away.

To add length to a pattern for a casing (figure 7–4), use the seamline or hemline as your starting point. Add to the pattern piece the width of the elastic plus ⅜ inch (1).

Stitch side, center-front, center-back, or underarm seams. Trim seam allowances to ¼ inch in casing area. Turn up casing allowance and press. Turn under raw inner edge ¼ inch and pin casing in place. Stitch close to turned-under edge, leaving an opening to insert the elastic (2).

Cut elastic the length of your body measurement, plus 1 inch. Use a safety pin or bodkin to pull the elastic through the casing. Pin remaining free end of elastic to garment so it does not twist or pull into the casing (3).

Lap ends of elastic ½ inch and stitch securely (4). Stretch elastic to bring fabric into place. Stitch opening closed, stretching elastic if necessary (5).

Casings with a ruffle will add an elegant touch to long or short sleeves or necklines of soft dresses and blouses, or at the lower edge of a blouse. The ruffle, which should be about ½-inch to 1-inch wide, may affect the length of the finished garment. In most cases, the elastic will pull the fabric close to the body and garment length adjustment may not be needed. Just remember *proportions* are one of the most vital considerations for the full-rounded figure.

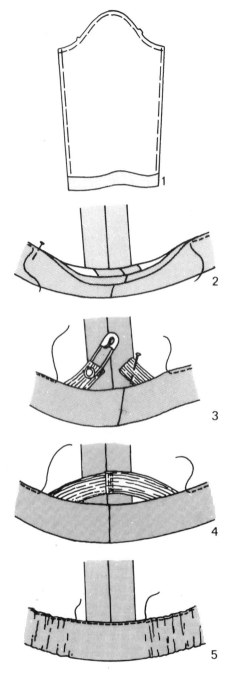

To adjust the lower or top edge of the pattern pieces, add twice the desired width of the ruffle, twice the width of the elastic, plus ¼ inch beyond the seamline or hemline.

When garment pieces are cut out, stitch all seams that cross the casing. Trim seam allowances to ¼ inch in the casing area. Turn up ruffle and casing along the proposed ruffle foldline. Press. Turn under raw inner edge ¼ inch and pin casing in place. Stitch ruffle layers together the desired width from the outer folded edge. Stitch inner folded edge in place to form casing, leaving an opening to insert the elastic (figure 7–5). Insert elastic and complete casing same as for plain casing (figure 7–4, steps four and five).

hemline, and press. Trim pressed raw edge to ⅜ inch above the fold. Pin bias tape over trimmed garment edge, placing tape about ⅛ inch above fold (figure 7–6). Turn in ends ¼ inch where they meet, for an opening. Stitch close to both folded edges of bias tape (1). Cut elastic the length of the body measurement; insert elastic through opening between ends. Join ends of elastic as for a plain casing (figure 7–4, step four). Slipstitch ends of tape together (2).

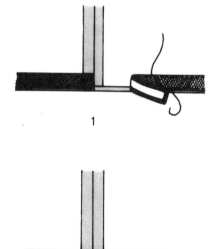

Figure 7-6

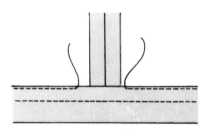

Figure 7-5

Applied casings at an edge are easier to make, as pattern changes are not required. Use single-fold bias tape in the desired width, and elastic about ¼-inch narrower than the bias tape.

Turn up the lower edge of the garment section along seamline or

Figure 7-4

Applied waistline casings away from an edge work well on a garment not fitted at the waist. The casing will gather the fabric around the body in small, even folds, and hug the body in a becoming manner. You can cut your own casing, or use purchased, single-fold bias tape.

To mark the position for a casing around your waist, tie a string around your waist over the garment as you are wearing it. Blouse the garment a bit above the string to allow for a graceful fit. Mark the garment along the string with tailor's chalk or safety pins. Remove string and transfer the markings to the wrong side of the garment, evening out the line.

To make your own casing strip from self-fabric (figure 7–7), cut a straight-grain strip the circumference of the garment, plus ½ inch, and as wide as the elastic, plus ¾ inch, piecing if necessary. Turn under both long edges ¼ inch; press. Self-fabric or purchased bias tape will be applied to the garment in the same manner.

For a continuous applied casing, center casing strip over the waistline marking and pin. Turn in ends ¼ inch where they meet, best over a seam. Stitch close to both long edges of casing (2). Insert elastic, cut the length of your body measurement, plus 1 inch, and secure as for a plain casing (figure 7–4, step four). Slipstitch casing ends together.

For an applied casing that ends at a zipper (figure 7–8), apply same as steps one and two (figure 7–7), but ending strip at the zipper seamline. Insert elastic with a safety pin or bodkin and stitch ends securely in place, about ¼ inch inside the zipper seamline, where the zipper stitching will fall (2). Complete garment as instructed by pattern (3).

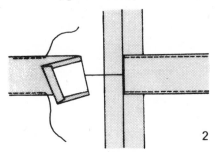

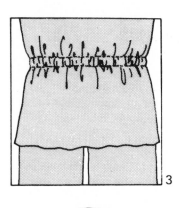

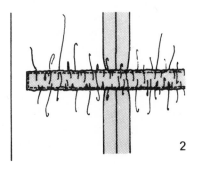

Figure 7-7

Figure 7-8

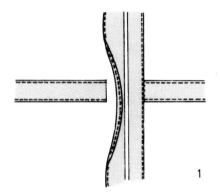 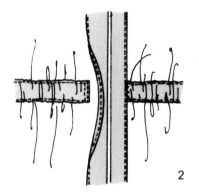 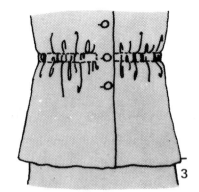

Figure 7-9

For an applied casing that ends at a facing (figure 7–9), apply casing same as step two (figure 7–7), but ending strip about ½ inch under the inner facing edge (1). Insert elastic with a safety pin or bodkin and stitch elastic securely in place across ends of casing. Slipstitch facing to casing strip (2). Complete garment (3).

Drawstring Casings

This classic fashion detail is currently enjoying a revival by today's designers. It is featured at waists of tops, jackets, skirts, pants, and dresses, with drawstrings tied at the center or sides. This is a great way to control garment fullness and allow for the expanding and contracting ample figure. Drawstrings may be self-fabric, cable cord, ribbon, or other trims.

To make a self-fabric drawstring (figure 7–10), cut a straight-grain strip the length of the measurement of the garment circumference at the waist, plus 12 inches, by four times the desired finished width. Fold the long raw edges under, making them meet at the center on the wrong side of the strip and press. Fold strip in half, with both long pressed edges even. Edgestitch folded edges together through all thicknesses (1). If desired, you can give your drawstring some flexibility with elastic. After you have made the drawstring, cut it in half. Sew each cut end securely to an end of a 6–7-inch piece of elastic that is the same width as your drawstring.

NOTE: After the drawstring has been inserted into the garment (use a safety pin or a bodkin), knot ends. Beads may be added before the knot is made. Narrow-hem the ribbon ends, or cut them on a diagonal to prevent fraying if you do not make knots.

To make openings for the drawstring, make machine-worked buttonholes, use large metal eyelets, or leave openings in seams. For buttonholes, baste a layer of fabric or interfacing, or use a piece of fusible interfacing, underneath the spot where the buttonholes will be made (1). Make buttonholes long enough to accommodate the drawstring, and about 2 inches apart (2). For metal eyelets, follow eyelet manufacturer's directions for application, placing them about 2 inches apart (3). To leave openings in a seam, stitch seam above and below the casing position, backstitching at both points (4). Press seam open before applying a casing. Stitch ¼ inch from the opening edges and across the top and bottom to reinforce (5). To prevent the drawstring from pulling out of the casing during laundering, stitch across the casing through all layers at side or center back seams (6).

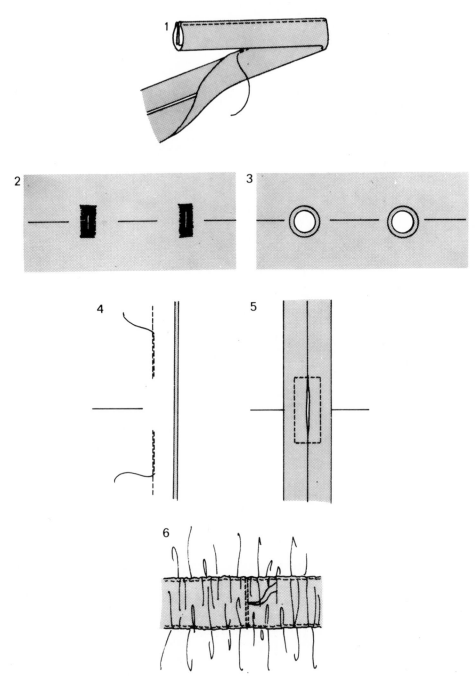

Figure 7–10

Drawstrings instead of elastic (figure 7–11) can be used wherever you have a casing. All you need to do is create openings for the drawstring as explained in steps one through four, figure 7–10, before you make the casing. Applied purchased bias tape casings will also work for drawstrings. See figure 7–4 for a plain casing (1) and figure 7–5 for a casing with a ruffle (2) to add to a favorite blouse, top, pants, skirt or jacket pattern. A drawstring casing at the waist of a dress or long top is a very pretty look (3). For a drawstring at a facing, stitch across short ends of casing strip as you stitch the long edges (4), after the openings have been made.

For a new twist, use two drawstrings inserted through openings at side seams. This is quite attractive when a casing with a ruffle is used (5), or as a belt substitute on a pull-on dress.

Drawstring casings on the outside of a garment need no openings (figure 7–12). Prepare a self-fabric strip as explained (figure 7–7). On the outside of the garment, center the strip over waist marking and pin. Turn in the short ends ½ inch, leaving a space about 2 inches free at the center-front of the garment, trimming away any excess strip length (1). Stitch long edges in place; insert drawstring (2). NOTE: Grosgrain ribbon may be substituted for self-fabric.

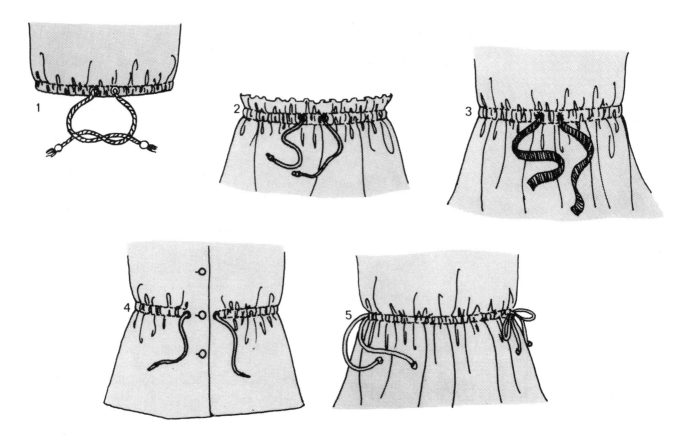

Figure 7-11

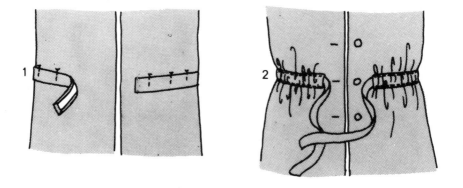

Figure 7-12

Facing Substitutes

A simple binding of self-fabric or a bolder statement with fold-over braid is a great substitute for neck and armhole facings. These bindings can change the total look of a dress, blouse, or top (figure 7–13). Narrow bias binding will help you glamorize an elegant sheer or lightweight dress or top (1), while fold-over braid will give a casual, sporty look to the same style garment when made in a heavier, more durable fabric (2).

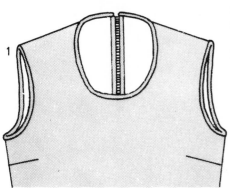

Figure 7–13

When using a binding or braid, do not cut out the neck and armhole facing pieces given with your pattern. For self-fabric binding, a ¼-inch-wide finished edge is the most popular choice. Purchased fold-over braid is usually ½- to ¾-inch wide.

Reinforce Opening Edges

To prepare neck and armhole edges for binding or braid, first stitch all garment seams (figure 7–14). Next, stitch ¾ inch from the raw edge to be bound, for reinforcement. Trim away the ⅝-inch seam allowance (1). NOTE: Neck and armhole edges will not fit you if the

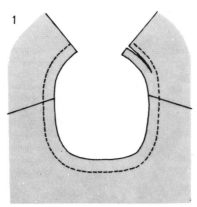
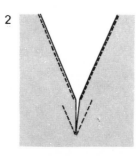

Figure 7–14

seam allowances are not trimmed away.

For a V-neckline or inward corners, prepare edges. Reinforce the point or corner with small (12–15 stitches per inch) machine stitches. Stitch about 1 inch on each side of point or corner, as shown, ¼ inch from raw edge, for ¼-inch-wide, self-fabric binding, or ½ inch away for fold-over braid of that width. Clip to inner point (2).

Self-fabric Binding

To make a ¼-inch-wide binding, cut bias strips 1¼ inches wide, the length of the neckline and armholes, plus 2 to 3 inches for finishing. Piece strips on the straight grain if necessary. To prepare the strips for binding, press, gently stretching the strip as you press to remove the slack, and pressing any piecing seams open (figure 7–15). Fold strip in half lengthwise, wrong sides together, and press gently (1). Open strip and bring raw edges in to meet the fold; press only outer folded edges. Refold, making lower edge a scant ⅛-inch wider than the upper edge. Press center fold gently (2).

To bind raw edges with a self-fabric bias strip, first shape the bias with a steam iron to match any curves on the garment. For an inward curve, stretch the two folded edges while easing the single-folded edge (3). For an outward curve, stretch the single-folded edge while easing the two folded edges (4). NOTE: Straight edges do not need to be preshaped.

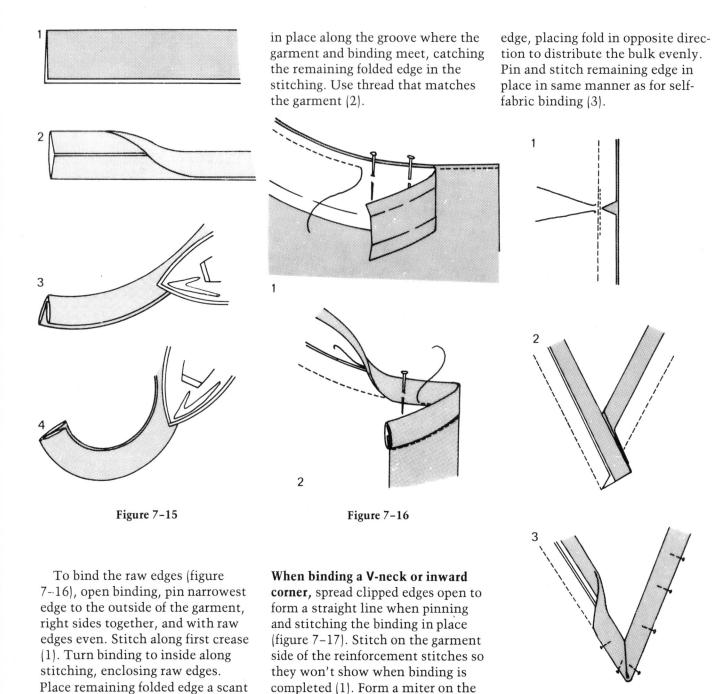

in place along the groove where the garment and binding meet, catching the remaining folded edge in the stitching. Use thread that matches the garment (2).

edge, placing fold in opposite direction to distribute the bulk evenly. Pin and stitch remaining edge in place in same manner as for self-fabric binding (3).

Figure 7-15

Figure 7-16

Figure 7-17

To bind the raw edges (figure 7-16), open binding, pin narrowest edge to the outside of the garment, right sides together, and with raw edges even. Stitch along first crease (1). Turn binding to inside along stitching, enclosing raw edges. Place remaining folded edge a scant ⅛ inch over the first stitching and pin. On the outside, stitch binding

When binding a V-neck or inward corner, spread clipped edges open to form a straight line when pinning and stitching the binding in place (figure 7-17). Stitch on the garment side of the reinforcement stitches so they won't show when binding is completed (1). Form a miter on the inside and pull the folds through the clip (2). Miter the inner remaining

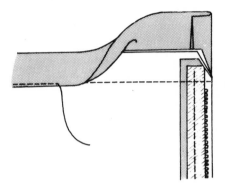

To finish binding over a zipper or other opening edge, turn under the raw end ½ inch. Pin and stitch binding in place, continuing up across end of binding (figure 7–18).

To join ends in a continuous strip for armholes and continuous necklines, start binding at a shoulder seam for the neck and underarm seam for a sleeve (figure 7–19). Turn under binding ½ inch, making fold even with the seamline. Pin (1). Stitch binding in place along crease.

Figure 7–18

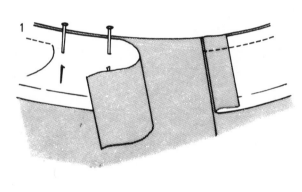

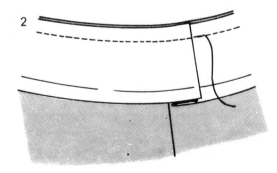

Figure 7–19

When you are about 2 inches from turned-under end, trim away excess binding so it will lap ¼ inch beyond the turned-under end (2). Pin and stitch remaining edge in place same as for figure 7–16, step two.

Fold-over Braid

Fold-over braid requires a slightly different technique than that used for self-fabric binding. Prepare garment edges as explained in figure 7–14. Shape braid same as for self-fabric binding, figure 7–15, steps three and four. To finish ends above a zipper, follow figure 7–18 and lay ends at a seam same as figure 7–19.

After the garment edge is reinforced, slip fold-over braid over the raw edge, placing the longest edge on the inside of the garment and the shortest edge on the outside. The reinforced and trimmed garment edge should be even with the inner crease of the braid (figure 7–20). Pin braid in place from the outside of the garment. Baste. Stitch close to the finished braid edge through all thicknesses on the outside of the garment (1).

For a V-neck or inward corner, spread the clipped edges open to form a straight line when pinning and stitching the braid in place (2). Form a miter on the inside and stitch in place through all thicknesses (3). Press fold flat and tack in place (4) for a smooth miter on the outside (5).

Finish ends above zipper or lap ends at a seam same as for self-fabric binding.

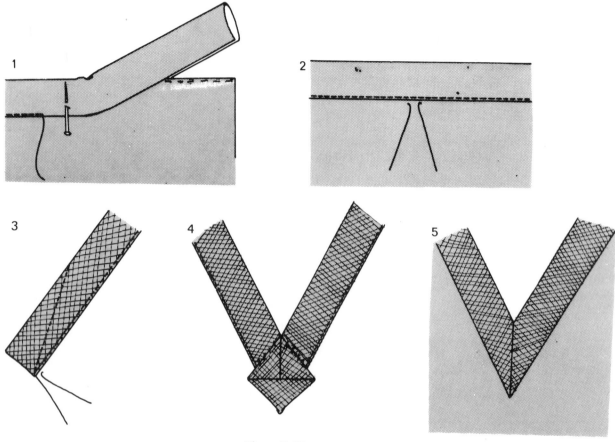

Figure 7–20

Gathers and Pleats that Complement

These two style features must be used with discretion on the ample figure. Both could add more bulk, but with a wise choice of fabric you will find them another way to add variety. See the pattern variations for gathers and pleats in chapter six, figures 6–14 and 6–15.

Gathers

Pretty, feminine folds of fabric can be made to work for your figure with the proper soft, drapy fabric (figure 7–21). A fabric that is crisp may cause the skirt to stand out away from the hips too much. If you have added gathers and the design and fabric are not performing exactly as you had envisioned, do not despair. To resolve the problem without reducing the circumference of the hem, the excess fabric at the waist and hips may be darted out.

Figure 7–21

Pin in darts as deep as required down to your fullest hip area while still retaining some gathers at the waist. When the fabric lies as smooth as desired, space the darts evenly around the body. Remove old gathering threads and stitch darts (1). Trim darts to ⅝ inch and press open. Regather waist seamline and complete garment.

Pleats

When selecting a pattern for a pleated skirt, you will find that single, inverted center-front and center-back pleats are the most flattering. Two or three pleats, front and back, can be attractive as well. Use soft fabrics for unpressed pleats and thin to medium-thick, crisp fabric for stitched and pressed pleats. Since all pleats involve three layers of fabric, you may want to trim away one layer after an inverted pleat has been stitched in place, to eliminate some of the bulk (figure 7–22).

Make the pleat as instructed, but do not topstitch the three layers together on the outside of the pleat. On the inside, open out the pleat. Keeping skirt free, and starting where the bottom of the topstitching would fall, stitch across the one pleat fold, one at a time, moving from pleat stitching to the fold. Backstitch at each end (1).

When both sides are stitched, turn pleat folds into position. Carefully split fabric along the pleat folds down to within ⅝ inch of your new stitching, and trim away this layer of fabric (2).

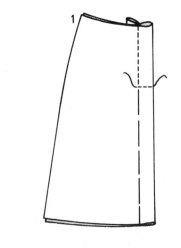

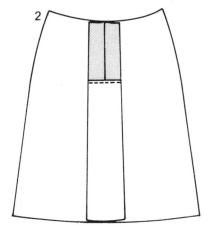

Figure 7–22

Becoming Ruffles and Flounces

These feminine charmers have been around for eons, it seems. Used for both garments and home furnishings, their names are sometimes confused. Ruffles are created from narrow strips of fabric or lace, usually gathered along one edge, and are most often used as trim. Flounces are much wider fabric strips that are gathered or pleated along one edge and are used as part of the garment rather than as a trim.

Ruffles and flounces should be used with discretion on an ample figure. The secret is not to overwhelm your body with ruffles or flounces in too many areas or in the wrong areas. Use a ruffle around the neck or at the hem but keep plain edges elsewhere. Ruffles around a short sleeve will call attention to a big arm, and ruffles around the lower edge of a blouse or top may emphasize hip girth. A flounce, however, may be used on a plain sleeve that ends just below the elbow or as a short sleeve in itself. Both a pleated or gathered flounce will look good at the bottom of either a floor-length or a street-length skirt. Make sure your fabric will support the weight of a flounce, so the silhouette will not collapse.

General Tips for Ruffles and Gathered Flounces

Cut ruffles and flounce fabric strips one and one-half to three times the length of the edge it will be sewn to. Use one and one-half the fullness for medium-thick fabric, double fullness for lightweight fabric, and a triple fullness for sheer fabrics. Some ruffles and flounces are best as a single layer of fabric, others as a double layer. There is no rigid rule about single vs. double thickness, other than preference. A double thickness gives soft fabric ruffles and flounces more body, but could make ruffles and flounces in crisper or heavier fabrics too stiff and bulky. For a double-thickness ruffle or flounce, cut the fabric twice the desired width, plus twice the width of the seam allowances to be used. Fold the fabric in half lengthwise, wrong sides together, with the folded edge replacing a hem. Cut a single-thickness ruffle or flounce the desired finished width plus seam and hem allowances. The ungathered edge of the ruffle or flounce will be hemmed.

Use straight-grain or bias strips for either ruffles or flounces. Allow extra length for seams when piecing strips (figure 7–23). At the sleeve hem, around a skirt, and at some neck edges, ruffles and flounces may be continuous. For a single-thickness ruffle or flounce, join the short ends. Press seams open and finish the raw seam allowances before hemming (1). On fine or sheer fabrics, you may want to join the ends in a French seam for a better finish. For a double-thickness ruffle or flounce, join the ends and press the seam open (2).

For a ruffle that ends at an opening, narrow-hem the end of a single-thickness ruffle (3). For a double-thickness ruffle, fold strip wrong sides together and stitch ends in a ¼-inch seam (4).

Gathering threads for ruffles or flounces should be made using your longest machine stitch. Stitch on the right side of the fabric for ruffles and flounces to be inserted in a seam, and on the wrong side for ruffles and flounces to be applied on

the outside of a garment. Since the bobbin thread is what you pull up to gather a ruffle or flounce, use heavy-duty thread or buttonhole twist on the bobbin to prevent thread breakage, especially for heavier fabrics. For lighter fabrics, make two rows of gathering stitches in the seam allowance. For heavier fabrics, you might try your widest machine zig-zag stitch over a cord of pearl cotton or similar material. Pull up the cord to gather the fabric. After stitching, remove the cord.

To help distribute the ruffle or flounce gathers evenly, divide the prepared strip into four or eight sections and mark with pins, and di-

vide off the garment seamline in the same manner. At the pin markers, stop and start gathering stitches to lessen the chance of thread breakage. Try to keep rows of gathering stitches less than 36 inches long. Match pin markers of ruffle or flounce to garment. Pull up gathering threads to fit, allowing extra fullness at outward corners and less fullness at inward corners as you distribute the gathers evenly. When stitching ruffles or flounces on top of the garment, rather than inserted in a seam, stitch on each side of the gathering threads so they can be removed easily after stitching is completed (5).

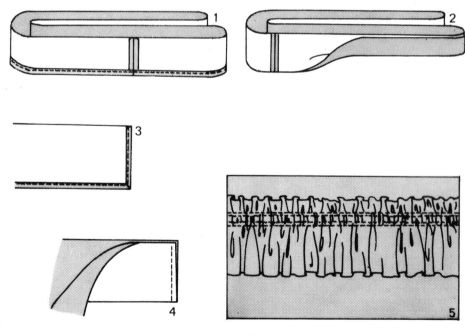

Figure 7–23

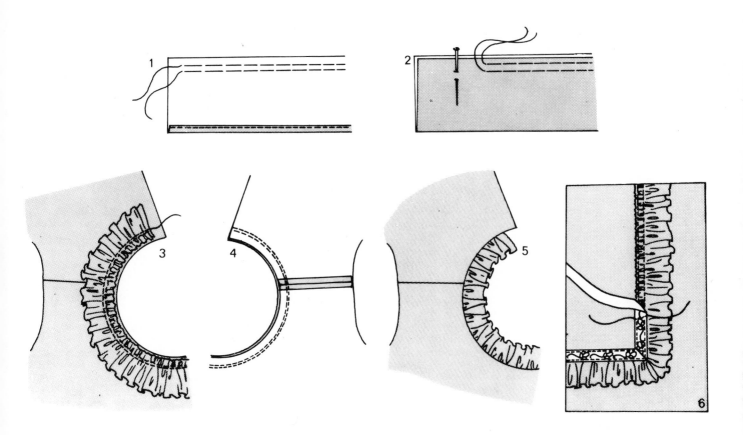

Figure 7-24

Single-Edge Ruffles

These ruffles are usually caught in a seam or held in place with a decorative trim (figure 7-24). For a single thickness, cut ruffle strips the desired width plus 1⅛ inches (⅝ inch for a seam allowance and ½ inch for a narrow hem) (1). For a double thickness, cut ruffle strip twice the desired width plus 1¼ inches for two, ⅝-inch seam allowances (2).

After ruffle has been gathered and hemmed, pin to garment; adjust gathers and distribute evenly. Machine-baste in place (3). Pin facing or other garment section in place, encasing the ruffle. Stitch from the garment side, next to machine basting (4). Trim and grade seam, clip curves, and turn right side out (5). Press the seam with the tip of your iron; do not press ruffle.

To attach a single ruffle onto the surface of a garment, pin ruffle in place, adjusting gathers evenly. Machine-baste ruffle in place. Press seam allowance flat; do not press ruffle. Trim seam allowance to accommodate band of trim, if necessary, for fit. Place band over ruffle seam allowance, covering the gathering threads. Stitch both edges of trim in place through all thicknesses (6).

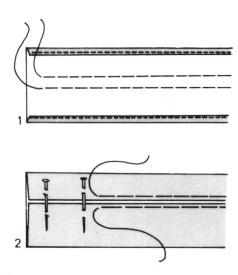

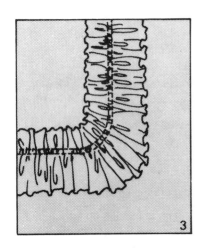

Figure 7–25

sired width plus 1 inch for two ½-inch hems. Narrow-hem both long edges of the ruffle strip, and short ends if it is not a continuous ruffle. Make two rows of the gathering threads ½ to 1 inch from one edge for the heading (1). For a double thickness, cut ruffle strip twice the desired finished width. To form ruffle strip, fold wrong sides together with cut edges meeting so the gathering threads will be ½ to 1 inch from one fold for the heading. Add gathering threads ⅛ inch from each cut edge (2).

Pin ruffle strip to the surface of the garment. Adjust gathers and distribute fullness evenly. Stitch in place alongside gathering threads as directed in figure 7–23, step five. For a double-thickness ruffle, stitch twice, with a row of stitching alongside each row of gathering threads, making sure that both layers of the heading and ruffle are caught in the stitching (3).

Double Ruffle

This style of ruffle is gathered with rows of stitching right down its middle (figure 7–26). For a single thickness, cut the ruffle strip the desired width plus 1 inch for two, ½-inch hems. Narrow hem both long edges and short ends if it is not a continuous ruffle. Make two rows of gathering threads in the center (1). For a double thickness, cut ruffle twice the desired finished width. To form ruffle strip, fold wrong sides together with cut edges meeting at the center. Add gathering threads ⅛ inch from each raw edge (2).

Pin ruffle strip to the surface of the garment. Adjust gathers and distribute fullness evenly. Stitch in place as directed in figure 7–23 step five. On a double thickness, stitch twice, with a row of stitching alongside each row of gathering threads, making sure that both layers of the double thickness are caught in the stitching (3).

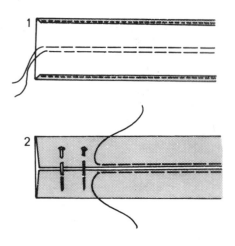

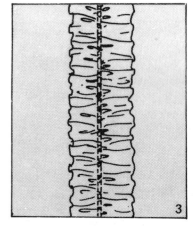

Figure 7–26

Ruffle With a Heading

This type of ruffle has two free edges, with the top edge a narrow heading, usually ½- to 1-inch wide and above the ruffle stitching. The ruffle portion can be any depth you desire (figure 7–25). For a single thickness, cut ruffle strip the de-

Gathered Flounce

The gathered flounce is made exactly like a ruffle but is much wider, usually 10- to 16-inches deep. Remember, it creates a horizontal line and must be in the right proportion for your figure.

When adding a flounce to a sleeve or skirt, which adds extra length, the pattern should be shortened. Draw a line on the pattern up from the hemline the desired depth of the flounce. Each style flounce will need a special hem allowance on the garment. For the seamed flounce, draw a second line 1½ inches below the first line, and for a flounce with a heading, draw the second line ⅝ inch below the first line. For both styles, turn back the pattern along the second, lower line. This will be your new cutting line on this garment section.

When cutting a flounce (figure 7–27), follow the General Tips for Ruffles and Gathered Flounces, at the beginning of this section in figure 7–23, to make seams and gathers.

For a seamed flounce, follow cutting instructions for a single-thickness ruffle figure 7–24, steps one and two. Gather and pin flounce to garment at garment's lower edge, right sides together, placing bottom gathering line 1½ inches in from the cut edge of the garment, with raw edges facing the same direction. Stitch. Press only the seam allowance flat. Turn under raw garment edge ¼ inch. Turn edge down over gathered seam allowance and stitch turned-under edge in place, through all thicknesses, keeping garment and flounce free (1). Turn flounce down into place.

For a flounce with a heading, make the heading a double thickness. Plan for a heading ½- to 1-inch deep, plus ½ inch for gathering threads. The heading will extend above the hemline—the first line you drew on your pattern. Cut the flounce the desired width, plus ½ inch for a narrow hem, plus double the heading width, adding another ½ inch for the gathered area. Example: For a 10-inch-deep flounce with a 1-inch heading, you will need a strip 13¼-inches deep (10 inches for flounce, ½ inch for hem, 2¾ inches for heading and gathering threads).

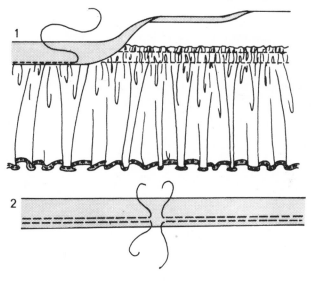

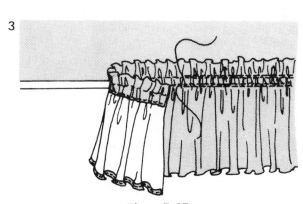

Figure 7–27

Make flounce length the desired fullness according to the fabric and garment circumference.

Turn down the top edge to form heading (1½ inches for a 1-inch heading) and press. On heading, make two rows of gathering stitches ¼ inch apart, starting ⅞ inch down from the folded edge. Narrow-hem the remaining raw edge of flounce (2). Turn up raw garment edge ½ inch; press. Pin and stitch flounce to garment, with lower row of gathering threads ⅛ inch above folded garment edge, stitching through all thicknesses as shown in figure 7–23, step five (3).

Pleated Flounce: This style of flounce may be 10 to 16 inches deep, depending on the proportions needed for your figure, as the seam will create a horizontal line. To adapt your pattern, draw a line up from the hemline the desired depth of the flounce. Draw another line ⅝ inch below the first one to create a seam allowance. Turn back the pattern along the second line for your new cutting line.

For a pleated flounce, you will need a strip about three times the measurement of the garment edge where it will be sewn. To find out how much is actually needed, cut strips of paper (tissue or newspaper) and tape together at short ends. Make box pleats or knife pleats 1 to 2 inches deep, depending on how full you want the flounce to be. Cut enough strips to pleat around the entire edge; this will be your pattern. Unpleat the paper and use it to cut fabric this length, allowing extra for seam allowances for any necessary piecing of the strip. To the desired finished depth, add 1⅝ inches for a ⅝-inch seam allowance at the top and a 1-inch hem.

To make pleated flounce (figure 7–28), hem lower edge by hand or machine, finishing raw hem edge as required for your fabric (1). Form box pleat and inverted pleat combination (2) or knife pleats (3) in flounce, following your paper pattern. Press pleats flat, making hem edges even; baste upper edge. Pin and stitch flounce to garment, right sides together and with raw edges matching. Turn flounce down and press. On the outside, stitch ⅛ inch from seam to help support pleats (4).

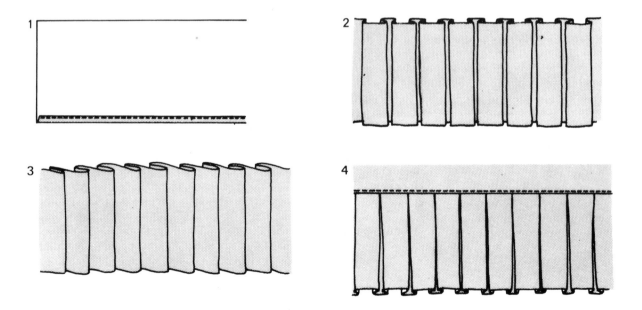

Figure 7–28

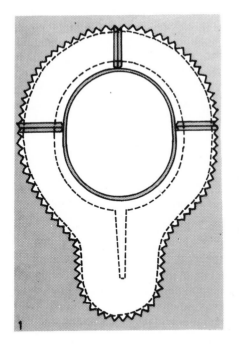 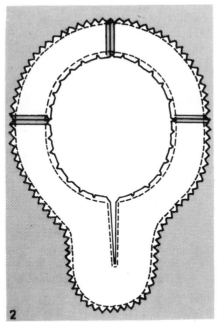 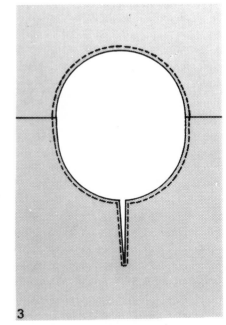

Figure 7–29

Special Openings

These little designer touches will allow you to change necklines and sleeves into high-fashion features. You can make slits, squares, rectangles, and keyhole openings on plain necklines, adding one of the special closures, if desired—ties or a tab. Many of the ideas shown here can be used for both necklines and sleeves. If you are planning to change the plain, high neckline of a dress or top, keep in mind that in addition to the neck opening as is, you will need about six inches added in the form of a slit, or another style opening to allow the garment to slip over your head easily, especially if you plan to eliminate any zipper and make the garment a pull-on style. For sleeves, there is no problem with getting them on the arms, but to keep design details in scale with your body, make new openings 1 to 3 inches deep.

Plain Openings

For this type of opening, a facing is necessary for a neckline and an extended hem allowance is needed for sleeves. Make these facings or hem allowances 1½ inches longer than the proposed length of the opening; for a neck facing, allow a 1½-inch extension on each side of the opening. When using interfacing around the opening, make it the same size as the facing and the extension or hem.

For a slit neck opening, cut facing with an extension at least 7½ inches long, or longer if a slit deeper than 6 inches is desired (figure 7–29). Stitch shoulder and back seams in garment and facing. Clean-finish outer raw edges of facing as your fabric requires. Draw a line down the center-front of the facing at least 6⅝-inches long (6 inches for slit length, ⅝ inch for neck seam allowance) for the slit. Pin facing to neck edge and along the center-front of garment, right sides together. Stitch neck edges to ¼ inch of slit line. Pivot stitching and taper stitching to the end of the line, taking one stitch across the point, and continuing tapering the stitching back up toward neck edge, stopping ¼ inch away from the slit line at the opposite side on the neck-seam allowance (1), continuing neckline stitching. Slash between stitching to point. Trim and clip neck seam (2). Turn facing to inside and press. Edgestitch or topstitch ¼ inch away from edge to prevent facing from rolling to the right side of the garment (3).

For a slit sleeve opening, increase the hem allowance as explained in Plain Openings. Sew sleeve seam. Fold up hemline to the outside of the sleeve and pin (figure 7–30). Draw a line from the hemline to the desired length of the slit. The center of the sleeve is the best position. Starting at the hemline, stitch ¼ inch from one side of the drawn line, tapering to end of line as for the slit neck facing. Take one stitch across the point and taper stitching back to lower edge, ending ¼ inch away from the line. Slash between stitching (1). Turn hem to inside and press. Complete sleeve, sewing hem in place by hand or machine (2).

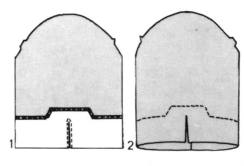

Figure 7–30

For a keyhole neckline, cut facing with an extension as directed in Plain Openings. Use a small glass or other round object to draw the rounded end of the opening, centering the curve over the center-front of the facing (figure 7–31). Starting ¼ inch on each side of the center-front, draw a tapered oval to complete the keyhole opening. Stitch garment and facing seams. Clean-finish outer edge of facing as your fabric requires. Pin facing to neck edge and along the center-front of garment. Stitch neck edge, pivoting stitching at corners and continuing along drawn lines (1). Trim seam to ¼ inch and clip curves (2). Turn facing to the inside and press. Topstitch ¼ inch away from edges or edgestitch to hold facing in place (3).

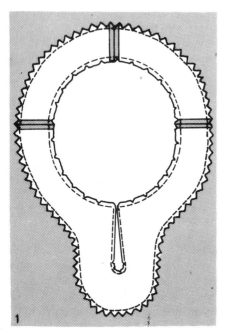
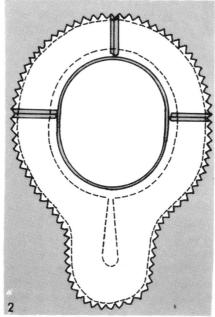
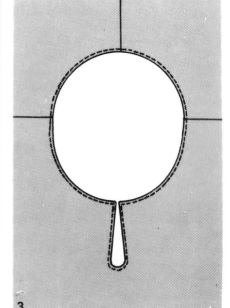

Figure 7–31

To add a button tab to the slit or keyhole openings (figure 7–32), also draw a center-front line on the garment as for the facing or on the right side of the sleeve where the slit will be. Cut two strips for each tab, 1½ inches wide and 2½ inches long to be used with a ½-inch button. Place tab pieces right sides together and stitch ¼ inch from the two long edges and one end. Trim corners (1). Turn right side out and press. Make buttonhole in finished end (2). Cut facing and hem allowances as explained in figures 7–29 and 7–30. Baste tab to the right side of the neck or sleeve; place one finished edge alongside the neck seamline or planned hemline, with raw edge along the drawn slit line (3). Complete slit as instructed for slit necklines or sleeves with slits, making sure the tab is caught in the slit stitching. Turn neck facing (4) or sleeve hem allowance (5) to the inside and press. Sew on button and complete garment.

Openings With Ties

This is an attractive way to finish an edge and stylize it at the same time. Use square, rectangular, or slit openings on a neck or sleeve. For the neck trim and ties, you will need a straight strip of self-fabric 2¼ inches wide and the length of the neck edge, plus 12 inches for two, 6-inch-long tie ends, or plus 6 inches for two, 3-inch tie ends. If your garment has slightly puffed sleeves, this is an especially appropriate sleeve finish. For sleeve tie closures, you will need a straight strip of self-fabric 2¼ inches wide

and the length of your arm circumference, plus 12 inches for two, 6-inch-long tie ends, or plus 6 inches for two, 3-inch tie ends.

To make a square opening for ties, cut a piece of fabric 4 inches wide and 4⅝ inches deep for a facing (figure 7–33). Draw a stitching line 1 inch away from the two long sides and the top edge. Center facing over center-front of garment or center of

sleeve, right sides together, and pin. Stitch along stitching line, pivoting at corners (1). Trim seam to ¼ inch; clip to stitching at corners (2). Turn facing to inside and press. Turn under remaining top and side raw edges of facing ¼ inch and edge-stitch in place (3). Complete neck or sleeve edge with trim and tie closure, figure 7–35 that follows the rectangular opening next described.

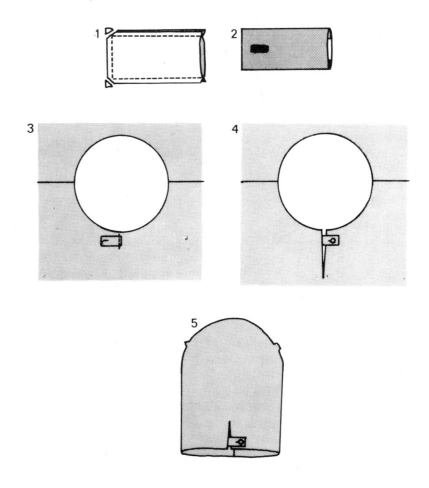

Figure 7-32

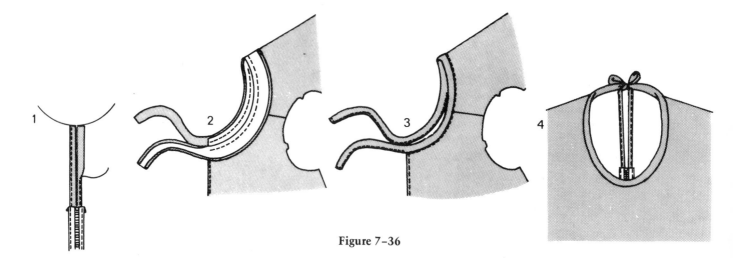

Figure 7–36

the seam, catching the binding edge underneath and stitching other tie-end edges together in a continuous seam (3). Make knots at end of ties and tie into a bow (4).

Wrap Skirts

This style is one of the greatest designs for large women to come along for a very long time. Wrap skirts are so easy to wear, and because of their adjustability they are a blessing to many women. Those who are troubled by bloating or water retention, or who at times cannot stand anything tight around the waist, have adopted the wrap skirt for its comfort and good looks.

On figures with large hips or thighs, the skirts do not always hang well across the back. A simple way to remedy this is to add 1¼ inches to the back-wrap pattern piece about 6 inches from the outer edge, or where the center-back is located. Slash and spread the pattern apart at this point, and tape in place over tissue or other paper. Clip-mark each side of the added width. After the skirt has been cut out, make a 7⅝-inch long dart ⅝-inch deep, starting at the waist, and placing it between the clip. Stitch, tapering dart to a point at the lower end. These darts give the added shape needed for the fuller figure across the back.

Skirts Without a Pattern

Thinking creatively about sewing for your ample figure should take you in a new, exciting direction. Skirts, very flattering garments for large sizes, can be made up quite easily without a pattern. In the preceding pages of this chapter, you will find instructions for elasticized and drawstring casings, and ruffles and flounces, along with the gathering information needed for these skirt styles. The skirts shown here are easy to make and allow for expansion. They will become valuable assets to your new, fashion-conscious image.

Drawstring Waist Skirt With Pleated Flounce

Three large, straight strips of fabric for skirt and flounce and two narrow, long ones for drawstrings are all that is needed to make this skirt (figure 7–37). Make it in a fairly soft fabric such as broadcloth, challis, flannel, or linen. Use your hip measurement plus 4 inches for wearing ease (due to the straight line of the skirt) for the *total width* of the fabric, using the desired finished length to estimate necessary yardage. Divide your *total width* in half for front and back widths, adding 1¼ inches to each piece for ⅝-inch seam allowances at each side. For length of the main skirt sections, first *subtract* 12 inches from your desired finished width to accommodate the flounce. Then, add 4¾ inches—4⅛ inches for a waist casing with a heading plus ⅝ inch for a lower edge seam allowance—to give you the length you need to cut each panel.

To find the width of the flounce, first make a paper pattern as shown in figure 7–28. Cut fabric the length of the paper pattern, plus seam allowances for any necessary piecing, by 13⅝ inches deep (12 inches for the flounce, ⅝ inch for an upper seam allowance and 1 inch for a hem). Also cut two drawstrings, each 4 inches wide, by the measurement of your waist plus 12 inches.

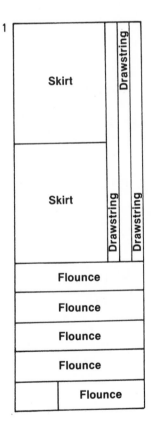

Figure 7–37

A diagram for 44- to 45-inch-wide fabric would look like this (1).

Cut out skirt sections as indicated, piecing flounce where necessary. Stitch top section of skirt together at sides, leaving a 1-inch opening in the seam on each side, 2½ inches down from the top. Press seams open and stitch around opening, through all layers, to reinforce. Turn down top edge 2 inches and press. Stitch ½ inch from fold. Turn under remaining raw edge ¼ inch. Press, and stitch in place, forming the casing (2). Make 1-inch hem in flounce and pleat (see Pleated Flounce, page 99). Stitch flounce to skirt, right sides together (3). Make drawstrings and insert one drawstring through each opening, entering and exiting at the same opening, using a safety pin or bodkin. Tie drawstrings into bows, adjusting skirt to fit your waist (4).

Elasticized-Waist Skirt With Three Gathered Tiers

This skirt, now a time-honored classic, is composed of three strips of fabric with gradually increasing circumferences (figure 7–38). It looks best in soft fabrics such as broadcloth, voile, gauze, or even lightweight denim.

Divide your desired finished length by three to find the depth of each tier. For the top tier, add 3⅛ inches to its depth, for a 1-inch casing, and a ⅝-inch seam allowance at the lower edge. The first tier's circumference should be your hip measurement plus 4 inches for wearing ease, plus the seam allowances needed for any piecing. The middle tier will need 1¼ inches added to its depth, for two, ⅝-inch seam allowances. Make the middle tier's circumference one-and-one-half times fuller than the top tier plus any necessary seam allowances. Also add 1¼ inches to the depth of the bottom tier, for a ⅝-inch seam allowance at its upper edge and a ⅝-inch hem. Make the bottom tier's circumference one-and-one-half times fuller than the middle tier, plus seam allowances as needed. To avoid errors, make a diagram of the skirt sections before you cut, writing in the dimensions of each piece

for easy reference and to help you estimate yardage. A diagram for 44-to 45-inch-wide fabric would look like this (1).

Cut out the skirt sections following your diagram. Stitch top tier pieces together, forming a continuous strip. Turn down top edge 1½ inches and press. Turn under raw edge ¼ inch and stitch in place, forming a casing, leaving an opening to insert elastic. Insert elastic and complete casing (2). Stitch middle-tier pieces together, forming a continuous strip (3). Stitch bottom tier pieces together, forming a continu-

ous strip. Turn up the bottom edge of the bottom tier ⅝ inch and press. Turn under raw edge again ¼ inch and stitch in place, forming a narrow hem. Add two rows of gathering threads to the top edges of the middle and bottom tiers (4).

Divide lower edge of top tier and upper edge of middle tier into four or eight even sections, marking with pins. Matching pin markers, pin middle tier to the top tier; adjust gathers, distributing evenly, and stitch. Join bottom tier to the middle tier in the same manner (5).

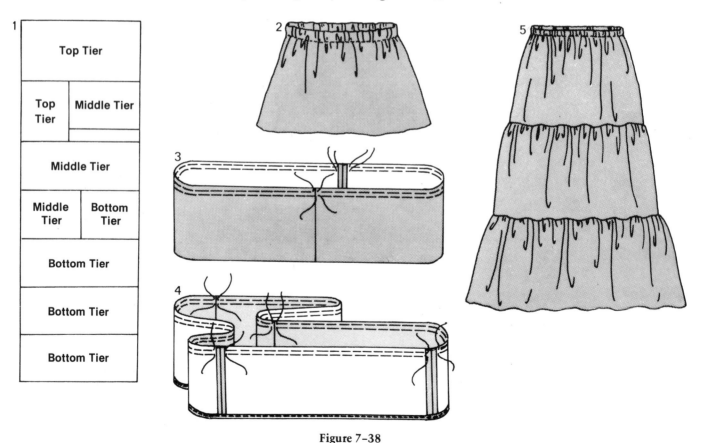

Figure 7–38

8

Fashion-Wise Accessories

Accessories can be the crowning glory to a handsome ensemble. Starting from this day forward, you should be keenly aware of just how those colorful accents will elevate your spirits and perk up your wardrobe. What you wear on your head, around your neck or waist, the purse or handbag you carry, and the shoes on your feet should all be used to help create the correct balance and proportion for your figure. I have seen women wearing beautiful, becoming outfits spoil their appearance with cheap, fussy, or poorly designed accessories. In most cases, it is better to have fewer items of better quality, rather than many inferior or inappropriate accessories.

For large women, it is especially important to *feel* well turned-out in every particular. This sense of well-being gives you self-confidence and an aura of attractiveness—truly invaluable assets. That is why your total costume, including all your accessories, deserve your undivided attention.

Hats

Now that hats are coming back into fashion, look for styles you can wear that complement your style. Until now, you probably only covered your head when the weather was cold, maybe with a scarf knotted under your chin or a knitted cap pulled over your ears. But no more. Think of hats as fashion items, special accessories that will turn a good outfit into a glamorous one.

A word of caution, however. Never select a hat by looking into one of those mirrored stands on the store counter. They were made only to frame your face and highlight your features. Instead, stand in front of a full-length mirror. A hat must sit firmly on your head, and will cover some of your hair. Do not simply perch it on top of your hair; neither your face nor the hat will look good (figure 8–1).

A hat with a brim looks good on most women, whether it is a fedora, derby, western, Spanish, or other brimmed styles. The width and tilt of the brim can work for or against you. The crown height must be considered as well. The general rule for brimmed hats is: the larger and taller a woman is, the wider the brim and the higher the crown may be.

Figure 8–1: Select accessories—hat, gloves, handbag, and shoes—that will help maintain a pleasing image that is balanced and in becoming proportions.

But if you have a large head, do not overwhelm it with a huge brim. Choose a brim that is a bit smaller to keep your head in scale with your body. Face shape also influences the way a woman looks in hats. Broad, wide, or round faces are better balanced with wider brims, while long and oval shapes look best in smaller brims.

Berets, pill boxes, and other small hats or head coverings will surely perk up your total look, but wear hats with a becoming hairstyle and suitable clothing. Hats are not meant to hide—they are meant to complement.

Scarves

These lovely bits of color must be worn with care. For most large women, scarves have a tendency to create an illusion of a shorter neck, making the head look smaller. Scarves worn around the neck and under a coat or jacket should not be worn ascot-style unless they are made of very thin fabric. Otherwise, your neck will seem to disappear into your body.

A scarf should not be worn close around the neck. To carry off this accessory on an ample figure, you should have a long neck, and the fabric should be soft and fluid. You can, however, tuck the scarf under the collar of a garment that has pronounced vertical or princess lines, or nearly vertical curved seaming. A warm, wool scarf, worn in this manner, will serve two purposes. It will add a slenderizing interest to a coat and will be available to keep your neck warm on cold windy days. Long, soft, thin scarves may be knotted low, near the bust (except on top-heavy figures) for a long, sleek look.

The choice of color in a scarf can be important. If you cannot match the color of a dress or suit in a chiffon or silk scarf, it is best to choose another color that will not contrast, but will harmonize with your outfit. Geometric or printed scarves have to be chosen with discretion, and should be worn with solid-color clothing so the scarf does not scream for attention or detract from a well-put-together appearance.

Jewelry

Put your jewelry to work to create an exciting, vertical lengthening interest for the top half of your figure. Most large women have a broad expanse of body at the top that can benefit from the illusion of sleekness. Start with a flattering neckline, such as a V-, scoop, or U-shape to form a pleasing focal point that will show off your favorite jewelry, as well as complement your face and hairstyle.

Earrings may be used to suggest length on a square or round face, and width on an oval or rectangular face. Select narrow, vertical shapes for earrings to add length, and large, rounded, or chunky ones for width. A triangular face will require careful attention to select earrings that are the best shape and size to counterbalance the narrow forehead with the full jaw and cheeks. Keep earrings small, preferably not dangling types. A broad forehead with a pointed chin is another challenging facial structure. For this shape, large geometric, rounded, or chunky styles can balance the face.

Ornate chokers are not usually flattering to a short, thick neck. Fine gold and silver chains are a good choice if you want to add interest to an open neckline. A small, dangling jewel or charm is an added plus when used along with those delicate chains. When wearing other types of short necklaces as a neckline filler, keep them as unobtrusive as possible, so they harmonize with the rest of your outfit instead of being in sharp contrast.

Bateau and high, rounded necklines will give you an uncluttered area to display your most complementary long necklaces, pins, or brooches. (See necklines in chapter 2.) A beautiful strand of opera-length pearls or other necklace similar in length, worn on a dark-colored dress is very chic and will be very flattering. Longer necklaces help create lines down the center of a bodice that cause the eye to move vertically instead of horizontally. A line of small pins or an elongated brooch placed on one shoulder will also add a vertical line. Gold and silver chains with large links, ropes of fabric fibers, beads, shells, and other interesting materials made into long necklaces add contrasting or harmonizing interest that helps to make a short neck seem longer and balance the top half of an outfit.

Belts

To wear a belt or not is the question most large women ponder. Matching-fabric belts in 1- to 1½-inch widths are great figure-shapers for those with a relatively slender waistline. For other figures, they will only emphasize large hips or a thick waist. Contrasting belts should be in soft color tones or nearly matching your outfit in color. A leather belt should be in the same color as the garment, as these belts tend to be heavier and can make the body look heavier if they contrast the outfit.

Large women should experiment with belt colors and placement to find the most flattering line for figure balance. The rectangular or large-bust figure may find a belt worn several inches below the natural waistline more complementary, because it draws attention away from a thick waist or large bust. Women with full, round hip, square, or round figures may want to accent the top portion of the body and balance a garment with a fabric tie belt worn several inches above the waist or just below the bust to create a high-fitting look.

Purses and Handbags

These items are frequently identified improperly. Purses are small containers used for money and small personal items, while handbags are large enough to hold money, small purchases, a book, or even a small purse. For any size woman, purses and/or handbags should be used to help create balance. A small purse is often lost in the folds of a garment on a large woman, and does nothing for her outfit. Over-sized handbags that look like briefcases or overnight bags will not add to a handsome ensemble, but will make you look sort of like a packhorse. Select an appropriate size bag that will add a bit of interest in texture, shape, and color to your total look. Stay away from bright colors. Instead, carry bags of neutral colors that blend with your clothing.

Select your bag for each occasion in front of a full-length mirror. Hang it on your arm, slide the handles or straps to your shoulders, see how it emphasizes or complements your figure as it is moved around. If you like to go dancing, little bags with long shoulder straps provide a welcome vertical line. Just make sure the bag is not too small, is in good proportion, and lies at the right spot near your waistline or on your hip (figure 8–2).

If your budget limits the number of bags you can buy, you would be best-advised to acquire one good, leather handbag for daytime use, rather than several low-priced ones. An all-purpose bag in a neutral color like black or beige, in a size that suits your body and your needs best, is a good investment. Shoddy plastic or cloth bags can cheapen whatever you wear. However, do not overlook handbags of simulated leather that look like the real thing, are of a good design and are well-made. Synthetic materials do have the advantage of easy care. These bags are washable and scuff-resistant. Good quality imitation leather bags are not cheap, but look good and may last as long or longer than a leather bag.

Figure 8–2: Wear appropriate shoes and carry a complementary purse for dancing or dress-up.

Shoes, Stockings, and Boots

Put your best foot forward with becoming shoes, stockings, and boots. For the ample woman whose legs and feet are not always her best feature, special care must be taken to ensure a total fashion look from head to toe. Stockings should not call attention to heavy or stocky legs. Keep shoes and boots polished and repaired. Large women wear them out faster, especially the heels. Examine all footwear periodically to make sure every pair is in good shape. Dirty, scuffed, run-down heels, or inappropriate shoe styles will project an indifferent feeling. Jogging shoes or sneakers are for active sportswear and should not be worn with a tailored pantsuit; clunky walking shoes are out of place with a soft, fluid dress; and cowboy boots or spike heels are inappropriate with a tailored designer suit or wool coatdress. Appropriateness is the key to wearing the right shoes with the right outfit.

Shoes

A big woman looks best in moderately high heels—up to two inches. Shoe styles and heel height should complement the costume and be in scale with the wearer's size. Spike heels 4 to 5 inches high will not be in proportion with your body, no matter how shapely your legs are. They will only succeed in making your legs look heavier when your whole image is viewed. An ample figure requires sure footing—extremely high heels will cause the body to pitch forward and you may stumble, seriously hurting yourself.

Because feet support the whole body, be nice to them and change heel heights from one day to another. It is good for your legs and back as well. If you must walk a distance, carry your high heels in your handbag and then slip them on before you make your grand entrance.

If you are *tall* and your husband or escort is about the same height, do not ruin an outfit with inappropriate flat shoes for his ego's sake. Wear a heel height that is in scale with *your* body (or the height suitable for the activity). You will look better.

The *short* woman should also select a heel height that fits the occasion. Too high a heel will make her look like she is walking on stilts, and flat heels may make her look childlike. Heels of up to two inches high work best.

The woman of *average* height, like tall and short women, should select a heel that will enhance her figure as well as her outfit. Be sure to match the style of the shoe to the function.

Pumps are the most flattering shoe style for most women, but many heavy women need the support of an ankle strap or even an oxford tie while walking. Flat shoes for anything other than active sportswear are not becoming to a large woman. For walking, choose a 1- to 1½-inch shaped or wedge heel. Large feet and thick ankles need the support of sturdy shoes, such as those that have a high vamp with elasticized front or side inserts, straps, or ties. Stay away from high wedge platform shoes, or dainty sandals, as they will emphasize the size of your feet and ankles.

Classically elegant pumps and sandals look best with a 1½- to 2½-inch heel. Heel heights and styles should complement your feet. For example, shaped heels add a sleek look. Barefoot sandals will need wider straps that hug and support the foot in a pleasing manner. Wedge heels, with or without thin platform soles, are one of the most comfortable shoe styles for the large woman. Look at your whole figure when selecting shoes; purchase the style that is the most versatile and complementary.

Stockings

Even the shade of your stockings can enhance or detract from your overall appearance. The large woman with heavy legs should select hosiery colors that match the shoes and complement her garment. Wear black, smoke, or taupe stockings with black, gray, or navy shoes in subdued tones that blend with your clothes. Light brown, tan, and other sandy shades look best with brown shoes. Wear light-beige and neutral-toned hose with bone, pastel, or white shoes. The fashion object is to use stockings that will not create an abrupt stopping and starting line at your skirt hem, or call attention to the size of your legs and feet. Inappropriately selected hose will seem to stand out so that they are one of the first things noticed about you.

The same guidelines apply to colored tights or textured stockings. The density of the tight's fabric will make its colors more outstanding. Even black tights may be too black for the shoes and garment, making them the predominant item of wearing apparel. Royal blue or red tights with black or navy shoes should be left to the very young, as this treatment will only emphasize large feet

or legs, even if the tights match another part of your outfit.

Strive for a monochromatic, high-fashion look. Wear dark stockings and shoes with dark clothes, and beige or neutral stockings with light shoes and clothing. Brightly colored shoes and stockings only can work well on a large person if the same color is used from head to toe with an ultra-sophisticated, understated garment.

Boots

For years, boots were utilitarian footwear, but now every fashion-conscious female has several pairs. The most practical type is a pair of sleek-fitting waterproof rubber or vinyl boots with a walking-height heel that is light-years away from the old black-buckle galoshes of yesterday. These new boots come in many shapes and colors and may be worn all year around in wet weather, with the addition of wool socks to keet your feet warm in winter. Save your leather boots for dry weather, unless they have been waterproofed.

Boots should be a subdued part of an outfit, not a predominate accessory. Natural leather and heavy, western styles look best with rugged outdoor clothes, and will not complement tailored or feminine indoor attire. In most cases, a large woman should wear boots that hug the ankles and legs in styles that end just below the knee in order not to add density to her legs. Some companies make wide-calf boots for women with that problem. Shorter boots can make your legs look

shorter and ruin the proportions of your outfit. Try on several lengths to see which type is most flattering. The best choice for a shorter length would be those that end just below the curve of the calf and have an arched top. Short boots should be worn with matching-color stockings if you wear the boots with a skirt. For pants, wear the legs tucked into your boots for a long, leggy look (figure 8–3).

Figure 8–3: Trend-setting large and lovely women select high-fashion hats, boots, and other accessories.

6

Ready-To-Wear:
Shopping...Altering...Restyling

Every day we are seeing more ready-to-wear clothing advertised for the big and beautiful woman. The styles are quite exciting and the selection is increasing rapidly, which means the garment industry is finally realizing that there are a lot of women in this country larger than a size 10. In this chapter, you will find tips on buying ready-made clothes, how to adjust them to fit your body in an attractive manner, and how to alter clothing you already have. The large-sized woman must select her clothes with care, making sure they flatter her and are neither too large nor too tight. Despite your size, you need never compromise style or fit.

After you have found a ready-made garment in a style that looks good, you will learn how to make simple alterations, if necessary, for a personalized fit. Smart-looking women want comfort as well as a good fit. If you have several ''good''

dresses in your closet that you will not wear because they are a little tight, you will learn several ways to restyle them.

Shopping can become a pleasure again, and you are bound to find some styles that are right for you in the many shops, department stores, or mail-order catalogs that carry fashions designed specifically for larger sizes. If you find one that needs some alteration before it will fit, you will not have to leave it on the rack or send it back. Now you will be able to make the necessary changes all by yourself.

Shopping for Ready-to-wear

If you have been disinterested in shopping for clothes, it may have been that you did not know how to select flattering garments, or that you weren't sure of your size range. There are two size ranges of ready-to-wear for large women—*half sizes* if you are 5'4" or shorter without shoes, and *women's sizes* if you are taller than 5'4" without shoes. You will learn how to measure yourself and how to use your measurements to find out your size category for purchasing garments.

Unless the clothes you spend good money on fit well, you will not be happy or look well-dressed. Knowing your size range and your figure-type needs will speed up your next shopping expedition or help you make wiser choices from mail-order catalogs. When you are in a store, do not hesitate to try on many different garments. It is one way to make sure the styles and size are right for you. When minor changes are indicated—hem length, taking in shoulders, etc.—see how the garment will look with the proposed alterations. Check if the hem is deep enough to let down, when necessary, and if the sleeves feel better when the armhole seam is pulled up to where it should be, or how the garment looks when other areas that are too loose are taken in. Look at the neckline construction when it gapes—plain neck finishes with facings can usually be changed quite easily, but designs with collars and bands may require extensive reconstruction. Match alterations to your skills. If you feel it is too much work, do not invest your valuable time and money in that particular garment, only to have less than satisfactory results.

Measuring For Ready-to-wear

Before going shopping or ordering from a catalog, you should know your height without shoes and your bust, waist, and hip measurements. These measurements are what manufacturers use to determine garment size. To find out how tall you really are, remove your shoes and stand against a wall with your head erect. Have a friend lay a ruler on your head, pushing your hair down flat against the skull. Make a pencil mark on the wall (or on a piece of paper taped to the wall behind your head) along the end of the ruler. Measure from the mark to the floor. Your height will indicate whether you should purchase half-size or women's size garments. Before taking your measurements, consider the following:

1. Start out with correctly fitted underclothes. (See Measuring for Undergarments, chapter 3.)

2. Have someone else measure you (it is usually more accurate), or measure yourself in front of a full-length mirror. Stand relaxed, your weight balanced evenly on both feet.

3. Measure carefully. Hold the tape measure snugly, not tight.

How to Take Measurements (figure 9–1)

1. Bust: Measure around your body at the fullest part of your bust. Make certain the tape is over your shoulder blades and straight across your back.

2. Waist: Measure around your body at the smallest part of your waistline.

3. Hips: Place the tape around the fullest part of your hips, usually 8 to 9 inches below your waist.

Move the tape up and down to find the widest point.

Your body measurements may not match the measurements manufacturers use—everyone is a little different. Purchase your garments in the size closest to your measurements, as wearing ease is allowed for every style. But do not take a bigger size just to be on the safe side. Too big a garment is as unattractive as one that is too tight.

Figure 9–1: Measuring for ready-to-wear sketch reprinted courtesy of Roaman's Mail Order, Inc.

To purchase the correct size, use the chart shown, courtesy of Roaman's Mail Order, Inc. The chart lists the standard measurements used by garment manufacturers. All garments have built-in wearing ease for comfort, so match your measurements as closely as you can to those on the charts. *Do Not* select a larger size for extra fullness to be used for wearing ease.

The rectangular and square figures can usually find their size without too much variation from the standard measurements. If you have a thick waist, there are a great variety of garments that have loose, flexible waistlines that will help you de-emphasize yours.

The figures with full, round hips or occasionally a round shape may need to purchase a larger size in order to fit the hips. Look for dress styles that do not have bust darts or bust fitting so you will not have to worry about bust alterations.

The large-bust figure may need a larger size to fit the top half of her body, so the dress or blouse will drape smoothly over the bust. Look for dress styles that do not have fitted hips.

ORDER DRESSES, COATS, SUITS, PANTS OUTFITS, JUMPERS, SHIFTS, GOWNS, ROBES AND LOUNGEWEAR

. . . in a half size if you're 5'4" or less without shoes
. . . in a women's size if you're taller than 5'4" without shoes

ORDER HALF SIZES	14½	16½	18½	20½	22½	24½	26½	28½	30½	32½				
ORDER WOMENS SIZES			38	40	42	44	46	48	50	52	54	56	58	60
If Bust Measures:	36 to 38	39 to 40	41 to 42	43 to 44	45 to 46	47 to 48	49 to 50	51 to 52	53 to 54	55 to 56	57 to 58	59 to 60	61 to 62	63 to 64
If Waist Measures:	29½ to 31	31½ to 33	33½ to 35½	36 to 38	38½ to 40½	41 to 43	43½ to 45½	46 to 48	48½ to 50½	51 to 53	53½ to 55½	56 to 58	58½ to 60½	61 to 63
If Hips Measure:	38 to 39	40 to 41	42 to 43	44 to 45	46 to 47	48 to 49	50 to 51	52 to 53	54 to 55	56 to 57	58 to 59	60 to 61	62 to 63	64 to 65

ORDER PANTS AND SKIRTS, KNEE-CAPPERS AND SHORTS

according to your hip measurement

ORDER WAIST SIZE:	30	32	34	36	38	40	42	44	46	48	50
If Hips Measure:	38/39	40/41	42/43	44/45	46/47	48/49	50/51	52/53	54/55	56/57	58/59

ORDER SHIRTS, BLOUSES, AND SWEATERS

in women's sizes according to your bust measurement

ORDER SIZE:	38	40	42	44	46	48	50	52	54	56	58	60
If Bust Measures:	40/41	42/43	44/45	46/47	48/49	50/51	52/53	54/55	56/57	58/59	60/61	62/63

When purchasing pants and skirts, *all five figure types* should go by hip size; for blouses, by bust measurement.

Fashion-wise Alterations

You have always wanted to be well-dressed in styles that complemented your figure, and nothing is more important to fashion than good fit. A garment may have flattering design lines and color, but if it has wrinkles and excess folds, or an uneven hemline caused by the shape of your body, you look dumpy. When this happens, the garment needs to be altered to achieve a smooth, sleek look. The fashion-wise woman will want to take the time to make any alterations she may need. You will be more satisfied with your new purchase when you have learned how to make it fit the contours of your body in a pleasing manner.

Hem Length and Uneven Hemlines

A simple hem adjustment may be essential to your new garment. This is unfortunately one area which many women tend to ignore. Too often, a full-figured woman will settle for whatever fits reasonably well. She will wear a dress or skirt just as it comes off the rack, in spite of the fact that only a small amount of time is needed to straighten the hem and make the garment totally flattering.

Select an appropriate hem length that will keep the balance and proportion of each outfit in scale for your figure. Do not follow the fads by raising or lowering your hemline each season when new fashions are introduced. Stay with *your* most flattering length. During the mini-skirt era, there were many style-conscious women who did not go along with this hem length. Few women—with the exception of the very young—could wear it well. Above-the-knee hemlines are *not* a good length for any of the five figure types, as shorter skirts tend to make a stout person appear heavier and broader.

A larger woman of *average* height will find a skirt hem ending at the crease at the back of the knee to about 1 inch below the kneecap the most flattering length for street wear. Coats may be about an inch longer.

Short women with ample figures should wear their skirts at the bottom of the kneecap. Too long a skirt will overwhelm a shorter woman, and too short a skirt will make her seem squat. A short woman needs as much of her leg showing below her knee as possible to keep her total outfit in proportion.

The *tall* woman will find it easier to maintain pleasing proportions, as she has the height to use as a counterbalance for her ample figure. The tall lady can have her hem at the bend in the back of the knee, or it can be as long as 2 inches below the kneecap.

No matter what your figure problems are, you should use your hem length to help create a dramatic fashion statement. The time spent finding the best hem length will help you camouflage those broad hips, thigh bulges, or misshappen knees, so that you will always be stylishly dressed.

The most common figure problems that will cause a hem to be uneven (figure 9–2) are the large buttocks that usually go with broad hips and large thighs. These figure flaws will make the hem shorter in the back (1). The round figure type, and those with a prominant abdomen, will cause the hem to arch up across the front of the dress (2).

To change the hemline, remove the thread that holds the hem in place. Press the hem area flat. Have a friend mark the new hem for you, or do as I do. Pin up several spots to the right length to make the hem even. Remove the garment and pin the entire hem smoothly, making it even from pin to pin, using your eye judgment. Put on the garment and check it again in front of a full-length mirror; make any changes needed. Do not be concerned if the hem allowance is much smaller or greater from front to back or from side to side; what is important is that the hem hangs evenly when you are wearing the garment. Trim the hem allowance an even distance from the hem fold, using the shortest area as the final hem allowance. Clean-finish the raw hem allowance edge the same way the original hem was finished. Pin hem in place. Sew hem to garment by hand, using a slipstitch, or machine blindstitch.

If you find yourself without an adequate hem allowance, you can face the hem. For this method, you will need about ¼ inch of fabric beyond the marked hemline, to sew on a facing.

Figure 9–2: Correct uneven hemlines for a smarter looking dress.

Hem Facing for Casual Garments: Use ½-inch-wide single-fold bias tape. Open out one folded edge of the bias tape and pin to garment, with raw edges even and right sides together. Stitch tape to garment along the crease on the tape. Overlap tape at ends. Turn tape to the inside and press, favoring the garment edge so the tape will not show on the outside of the garment. Pin and machine-stitch in place remaining folded edge of tape through all thicknesses.

Hem Facing for All Other Garments: Use 2-inch-wide bias hem facing. Open out one folded edge of hem facing and pin to garment, with raw edges even and right sides together. Stitch facing to garment along the crease on the facing. Overlap facing at ends. Turn facing to the inside and press, favoring the garment edge so the facing fabric will not show on the outside of the garment. Pin the remaining facing folded edge in place and slipstitch or machine blindstitch to garment.

Narrow Shoulders

The ample-figured woman does not always have narrow shoulders, but her figure may require a larger size dress, blouse, or jacket to compensate for over-sized hips. This fit problem (figure 9–3) in ready-to-wear garments will cause the sleeves to buckle and bind because they are not hitting the correct areas of the arms and shoulders (1). There are three ways to correct this problem.

Darts: Pull the armhole seams up into place over the arm hinges. Pin in darts, starting at the shoulder seam, tapering the darts to a point over bust and shoulder blades (2). Transfer darts to the wrong side of the garment. It will probably be necessary to open the shoulder seam to get a smooth dart line. Stitch darts and close shoulder seams, if required (3).

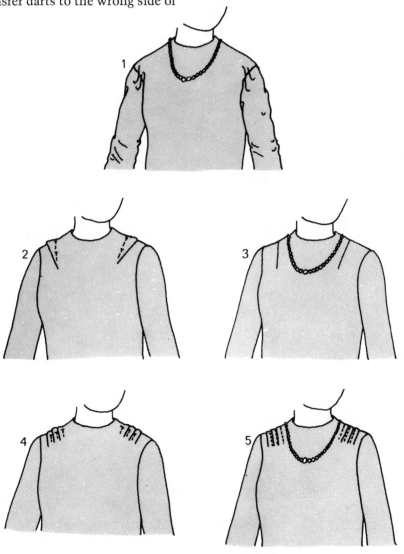

Figure 9–3: Reposition drooping shoulder seams caused by narrow shoulders or other figure flaws.

Tucks: Pull the armhole seams up into place over the arm hinges to see how much excess fabric you have along the shoulder seam. Pin several $\frac{1}{8}$-inch to $\frac{1}{4}$-inch tucks along the shoulder seam, extending the tucks 2 inches to 4 inches downward on each side of the seam ending at a pleasing spot above the bust and shoulder blades (4). You do not have to open the shoulder seam for these tucks. Stitch the tucks in place (5).

Shoulder Pads: On garments of heavier fabrics, such as jackets and some dresses, darts and tucks at the shoulders could be too bulky, so you might want to consider shoulder pads. While wearing the garment, insert the shoulder pads to get the correct placement. Pin pads in place. Hand-sew pads to shoulder and armhole seams, lifting any facings so pads are underneath the facings.

Narrow Back

Depending on your figure, you may have a narrow back across the shoulders and rib cage area (figure 9–4). The excess fabric is not very flattering if it bunches or billows outward, seeming to add bulk to your figure (1).

If there are no back seams, pin out the excess evenly on each side of your body, tapering to a point at each end, forming two long darts (2). Usually the darts will extend from shoulder seam to your high hip, crossing any waist seam. Transfer markings to the wrong side of your garment; stitch darts as fitted (3). For princess seams, take in both sides as needed. For a center-back seam without a zipper, take in as much there as you can. If the seam becomes too awkward, take in remaining fabric by making a dart on both sides of the center seam.

Gaping Back Neck

Lower necklines gaping across the back is caused by fleshy pads near the arms. Sometimes the front neckline is distorted as well (figure 9–5). The neckline may collapse or cause wrinkles across the back (1). To correct, make one large dart down from the back neckline to see how much fabric must be taken in (2). Stitch in ⅛-inch darts, as many as you need, each about 2 inches long. Taper them to a point, stitching through garment and facing as one (3). The front neckline may need the same treatment.

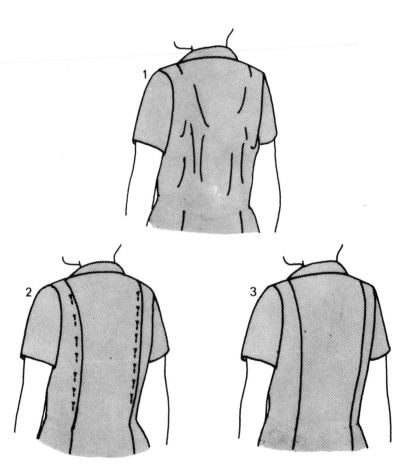

Figure 9–4: Eliminate excess fabric and wrinkles caused by a narrow back.

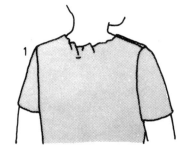 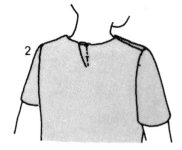 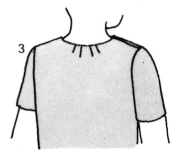

Figure 9–5: Smooth a gaping neckline with darts.

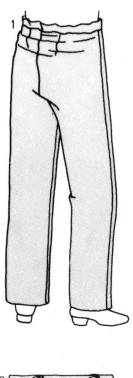

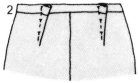

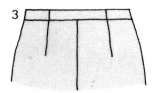

Figure 9–6: Fit a gaping waistband with darts to create waist-hugging pants.

Gaping Pants Waistband

So many women have this problem with pants and jeans. (This alteration will work equally well for a skirt.) The garments are not quite shaped the way many women are (figure 9–6). A woman may have a flat tummy and large buttocks, or be large all around the body in the hip area. The pants fit everywhere but across the back above the full hip (1).

To correct, pin in a dart on each side of the back, starting at the top of the waistband; taper to a point above the hips (2). Transfer markings to the wrong side of the pants and stitch darts through all thicknesses (3).

Baggy Crotch

Women of all sizes have this problem. The pants collapse right below the crotch in the back or seem to droop in front at the crotch. To get a smooth line, stitch in a deeper crotch curve, usually no more than ¼ inch, where the seam starts to curve up to the waist, either front or back, where you need it. Taper the stitching to the original stitching line at the inseam intersection.

Bust Dart Too High

Full-bust figures, young and old, often have this problem. The point of the bust dart ends an inch or more above the end point, or apex, of the bust, creating a rumpled look that could be uncomfortable as well.

Open the side seams and the bust darts. With the garment on, re-pin the darts lower, ending them about 1 inch away from the apex of your bust. Stitch darts and side seams.

Sleeve Length

Half-size women who buy women's size blouses often have this problem with wrist-length sleeves. If the sleeve has no cuff, you can just shorten the hem. For a straight or slightly flared sleeve with a cuff or band, pin out the excess length all around the sleeve (the sleeve should allow you to bend your arm without pulling on the armhole or cuff seam). Make one or several evenly spaced tucks above or below the elbow. To sew in the tucks on the right side, push the cuff end of the sleeve up into the sleeve to create an accessible foldline. Press tucks down toward the cuff.

Restyling Garments That Are Too Tight

If you are like most large women, you have several garments in your closet that fit a little too snugly, and you know you do not look your best when you wear them. If getting them to fit well involves more than letting out a few seams, there are several easy alterations that you can do to enable you to wear these neglected things again. Consider each suggestion carefully before starting.

Add a Panel

You may be able to find a commercial pattern with a panel down the front that will make this alteration easier. This will work on an A-line or sheath dress (figure 9–7).

Use new fabric that contrasts or complements, or recycle the fabric from another unwearable garment.

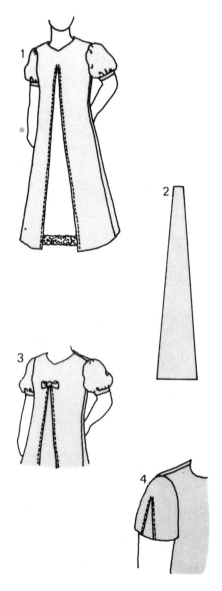

Figure 9–7: Restyle a tight dress with a panel that adds figure-flattering diagonal lines.

To prevent any distortion of the raw edges, staystitch ¼ inch from each side of the center-front line. Bring the side seams together if you have trouble finding the center-front line; the center-front will be the fold created by laying the side seams on top of each other. Decide how far up the panel will go, and stop the stay-stitching ¼ inch above that point. Split the garment up the center-front, between the stitching lines, keeping a ¼-inch seam allowance on each side (1). Try on the dress and spread apart the front to see how wide the panel should be. Make a triangular-shaped pattern, or adjust the one from a commercial pattern to your desired width, allowing for a hem (2). Stitch the panel in place, right sides together. Stop and start stitching at the upper point; do not pivot. Hem. For a finishing touch, add a bow that matches the panel (3).

Make the same alteration on short sleeves that are too tight (4).

Enlarging Bust and Armhole Area

For this change, you will need matching fabric. If the garment has a tie belt, it would be a perfect solution (figure 9–8). Often a wide hem allowance can provide the fabric. You can then face the hem as suggested in figure 9–2. When a garment is too small through the bust and seems to bind around the armhole, this can be corrected with a narrow fabric strip (1). The object is to use just enough fabric to make the garment comfortable, because you do not want to distort the proportions. The strip should be no wider than 2 inches. Carefully rip open the seam from waist to about 2 inches past the armhole seam. Spread seam and insert the strip, tapering to a point at each end as shown (2).

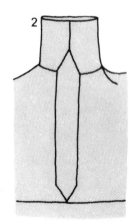

Figure 9–8: To give the needed extra fabric for a large bust, set in a matching strip at the underarm and side seam.

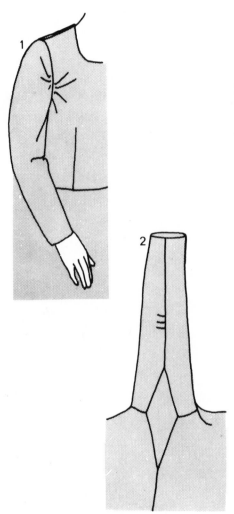

Figure 9-9: Use gussets to enlarge arm-holes that are too tight.

Enlarging Armhole Seam

When the armhole seam binds and is uncomfortable, it can be corrected with a diamond-shaped patch (figure 9-9). If you can find matching fabric, or fabric that is almost identical, you are in good shape. The fabric will, for the most part, be unseen, so it does not have to be an exact match. To add the patch, rip open the underarm seam only. Pin the sharpest point of the diamond at the intersection of the underarm and sleeve seam. Spread the underarm seam to accommodate the patch. Stitch. You may find it easier to stop and start stitching at each point of the diamond. The patch may be as wide as 3 inches when finished, where the armhole seam intersects the underarm, and up to 8 inches in length at opposite points (2).

Enlarging a Blouse with Lace

This is a decorative alteration as well as a practical one, but it is not for inexperienced sewers. Buy about 2½ yards of lace, 1-2 inches wide. The type and thickness of the lace depends on your blouse fabric. The wider the lace, the more width you will add to the blouse.

Wearing the blouse, pin-mark a line from the shoulder to hem of the blouse, going over the bust, on each side of the center-front. The lines will probably be slightly curved, but keep them parallel to the center-front below the armhole. Take off the blouse and draw in the lines with chalk or pencil, removing the pins. On the back, continue the lines down to the hem, keeping them parallel to the center-back below the armholes. Stitch ⅛ inch from the lines, on both sides. Cut apart the blouse on the lines, between the stitching. Open the shoulder seams for about ½ inch on each side of the cut. Overlap the lace ¼ inch, on the right side of the blouse, starting at the shoulder and moving down on each side of the cut, for front and back. The top of the lace should be even with the raw edge of the shoulder seam allowance. Topstitch or use a narrow zigzag stitch to sew the lace to the blouse. Stitch shoulder seams closed and hem or clean-finish lace at the lower edges. Should this alteration cause the sleeve to droop beyond the shoulder hinge, make a narrow dart or tuck on each side of the lace insert to bring the shoulder seam back to the original length.

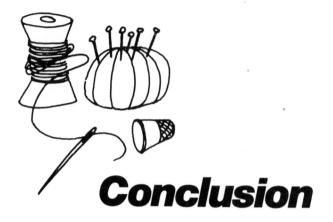

Conclusion

Beauty is a timeless and ageless concept. The large-size woman, young or old, can learn to pick becoming fashions for every occasion in her life. The greatest beauty aid is thinking positively about yourself. If you have a negative image of yourself, so will others. But if you feel good about yourself, that good cheer will certainly be noticed and appreciated. Take the plunge and dive into *Sewing Big* without hesitation, and come up with a workable plan for a figure-flattering wardrobe. The more you know about your figure, the more comfortable you will be in making fashion-wise decisions for your lifestyle. Pick your figure type and find help in each chapter to reinforce your commitment to be the best-dressed, most confident woman you can be.

Index